D1789487

Bandung
1955
Non-Alignment and
Afro-Asian Solidarity

Bandung 1955

Non-Alignment and Afro-Asian Solidarity

JAMIE MACKIE

EDITIONS DIDIER MILLET

Singapore · Kuala Lumpur · Paris

Text © **Jamie Mackie 2005**

Design and layout
© **Editions Didier Millet 2005**

First published in 2005
by **Editions Didier Millet Pte Ltd**
121 Telok Ayer Street, #03-01
Singapore 068590

www.edmbooks.com

Editorial Director
TIMOTHY AUGER

Assistant Editor
PASHA SIRAJ

Designers
TAN SEOK LUI
ANNIE TEO

Production Manager
SIN KAM CHEONG

Colour separation
by **SINGAPORE SANG CHOY**

Printed and bound in Singapore
by **UIC Printing**

ISBN 981-4155-49-7

Illustrations
Cover: Crowds outside the Hotel Homann during the Bandung conference;
the main assembly hall of the Gedung Merdeka during open session.
Frontispiece: The busy intersection of Jalan Braga in Bandung, with the
DENIS Bank building (1936) in the background.
Contents page: Delegates arriving at Kemayoran airport, with flags of the
participating countries flying.

To the memory of

Herb Feith and George Kahin,

the first and best of

Australian and American Indonesianists,

and Molly Bondan,

three good friends

who worked at Bandung in April 1955,

and helped us to comprehend better

what it was all about.

ACKNOWLEDGEMENTS

I am deeply indebted to the Museum Asia-Afrika in Bandung, especially to its Head, Drs Boedi S. Poerwohadikoesoemo, and to Ibu Budiantini S. Widjaja and Pak Dede Sutardi, for their most helpful assistance in allowing me access to its resources and for provision of photographs of AA Conference delegates, and other materials. I am also most grateful to Dr Roeslan Abdulgani, Secretary-General of the 1955 Bandung conference, for helpful discussions on various details, and to Ibu Retnowati Abdulgani-Knapp for her assistance in making those meetings possible and very pleasant. Others who provided valuable help of various kinds in Indonesia were Joan Hardjono, Frances Affandy, Thee Kian Wee and Tjoe, Juwono Soedarsono and Wuryastuti Sunario.

In Canberra and elsewhere in Australia I have had help of many kinds from Hugh O'Neill (for photographs of Bandung and advice on its architectural heritage), David Jenkins, Patrick Walters, Jim Fox, Robyn, John and Simeran Maxwell, Harold Crouch, Chris Manning, Martin Stuart-Fox, Bob Elson, Robin Jeffrey, John Legge, Liz Drysdale, Trish Van Der Hoek, Glen Luttrell, Ben Robbins and, especially, Ann Moyal.

My sincere thanks to all of them, and to those who have generously allowed us to reproduce their images, a full list of whom appears in the picture credits.

CONTENTS

LIST OF ILLUSTRATIONS

LIST OF MAPS

PREFACE

In 1955, the Bandung Conference of Asian and African Nations was seen in many parts of the world as a historically unique meeting of leaders of formerly colonised peoples, potentially the first of many such gatherings dedicated to the elimination of colonialism and the promotion of Afro-Asian solidarity. But no second or later such conference was ever held, for reasons which will be explored in due course in this book. Yet Bandung did give rise quite directly to the Belgrade Conference of Non-Aligned Nations in 1961 and to the later establishment of the Non-Aligned Movement (NAM), which has held frequent meetings since then and of which Bandung is acknowledged as its starting point and inspiration.

Bandung and non-alignment were therefore intimately connected, although the link between them was a tangled one. While the term had been in use beforehand (but not extensively), it came into widespread currency in the years following Bandung. Yet it was only one of the many issues that evoked discussion and debate there. It was not even an item on the conference agenda, nor does the term occur at all in the final communiqué, or in the *Dasa Sila Bandung*, the Ten Principles finally adopted (after intense argument). In fact, only three of the 29 participants, India, Burma and Indonesia, were openly committed to non-alignment, whereas the group of strongly aligned countries supporting the principle of collective security, which entailed support for anti-communist treaties such as SEATO, was much larger. The disputes between those two camps created great tension and drama in the later stages of the conference. (Some members of the aligned group even claimed to have achieved a big success by preventing the inclusion of any statement in favour of non-alignment in the final communiqué.) But several other countries swung strongly towards non-alignment in the years after Bandung, most notably Egypt under Nasser, and many of the African nations that achieved their independence in the 1960s, greatly swelling the membership of the NAM. Some of them tried hard to pull the movement in a strongly anti-imperialist direction. Paradoxically, many of the nations that had been opposed to non-alignment at Bandung had themselves become members of the NAM by the 1990s.

My aim in this book is to set the story of what happened at Bandung into its historical context for today's readers, who may be unfamiliar with the international background to it and the ideological climate in which it was held. I have not dealt with the NAM in much detail, apart from glancing briefly at its origins and the reasons for the failure of the Second Afro-Asian Conference at Algiers in 1965, which were closely intertwined issues.

The historic symbolism of Bandung and the high drama that attended it are not easily understood without some knowledge of its broader context. Valuable accounts of the conference were published long ago by Professor George Kahin, head of Cornell University's world-renowned Southeast Asia Program, and by Dr Roeslan Abdulgani, the Conference Secretary-General and Secretary of Indonesia's Department of Foreign Affairs, along with several others. But the assessments we make of it 50 years later are bound to have a different perspective. I hope my interpretations of Bandung's significance may help others to reach a better understanding of what it did and didn't achieve.

I am deeply grateful to the staff of the Asia-Africa Conference Museum in Bandung for making available to me its library resources and splendid photographs which bring the occasion so vividly to life. And I owe much to Pak Roeslan for his recollections, his writings and wise advice about it all, as well as for his valued friendship over many years.

TO MAKE 'THE VOICE OF ASIA' HEARD

'This is the first intercontinental conference of coloured peoples in the history of mankind', declared President Sukarno of Indonesia in his opening address to the Asian-African Conference in Bandung on 18 April 1955. It was also the first ever meeting of leaders of the newly independent nations of Asia—India, Pakistan, Ceylon (later Sri Lanka), Burma (later Myanmar), Indonesia, the Philippines, North and South Vietnam, Cambodia and Laos—or of Africa. The symbolism of such a meeting was very powerful at a time when great changes in world politics were occurring and much was being said all round the globe about 'the awakening of Asia' and the dismantling of old colonial empires, even though armed struggles to achieve independence were still under way in parts of Asia and only just starting to make headway in Africa.

The conference marked 'the political emergence in world affairs of over half the world's population', observed Prime Minister Nehru of India. 'This is the human race speaking', wrote Richard Wright, the famous black American, ex-communist author (overlooking, for rhetorical effect, the white, wealthy portion of the world), who wrote a lively account of the conference soon after, *The Color Curtain*. In it, he says he decided as soon as he heard about the gathering of so many once colonised and humiliated peoples that

> I had to go to that meeting. I felt that I could understand it. I represented no government, but I wanted to go anyhow… Only brown, black and yellow men…could have felt the need for such a meeting.

Issues to do with race, colour and religion were inevitably prominent at a conference of leaders of former colonies who wanted to bring about an end to colonial rule by white men throughout the world as soon and as widely as possible—and to its latter-day manifestations such as neocolonialism and imperialism. Amidst some fierce disputes on Cold War issues such as collective security pacts and 'new manifestations of

An illustration depicting a European colonial master lording over a 'coolie' worker.

colonialism', race did not become a major source of contention at Bandung, and was the one thing they were united on. Nationalism, anticolonialism and neocolonialism were prominent themes in the rhetoric there. And as Wright put it, 'a certain amount of repetition drove home the racial theme with crushing force'.

There was no one 'awakening of Asia' or 'voice of Asia', of course, or of Africa, but many, in various countries, over the course of a century or more. In India, its beginnings can be traced back at least to the 1820s, when the Brahmo Samaj was founded by Ram Mohan Roy, and to Rabindranath Tagore's later attempts to revive the Upanishads' ideals of education in his college at Santiniketan. In the Philippines, the first Asian nationalist martyr, Jose Rizal, was shot by a Spanish firing squad in 1896. China's famous May Fourth Movement in 1919 was almost a latecomer. Yet what Bandung signified in 1955 was that nearly all of them *had* awakened by then and were demanding that their voices should be heard. Independence was no longer just a dream. The old colonialist assertion that 'self-government is no substitute for good government' was no longer acceptable. The psychology that had

President Sukarno of Indonesia delivering his opening address at the Bandung conference.

The despised, the insulted, the hurt, the dispossessed—in short, the underdogs of the human race were meeting. Here were class and racial and religious consciousness on a global scale. Who had thought of organizing such a meeting? And what had these nations in common? Nothing, it seemed to me, but what their past relationship to the Western world had made them feel. This meeting of the rejected was in itself a kind of judgment upon the Western world.

Wright, **The Color Curtain**

sustained 'the white man's burden' and his (or her—the memsahib's) '*mission civilisatrice*' had become a thing of the past.

One purpose of the conference was to make 'the voice of Asia' heard in world affairs at a time of dangerous Cold War crises in Asia. Non-alignment between the two rival blocs of the major Western powers was a major concern for some, although the search for Afro-Asian unity and solidarity was also important. But fierce arguments took place between the advocates of non-alignment and the far larger group of Western-aligned countries opposed to it, all strongly anti-communist and anti-neutralist. So it was only with difficulty that the consensus expressed in the *Dasa Sila Bandung*, the Ten Principles, could be hammered together on those matters in the last, anxious hours of the conference.

The sense of Asian and African (AA) solidarity and the appeal of non-alignment were greatly enhanced at Bandung and remained potent ideals in both continents for many years afterwards. They became dissipated in the 1960s, and even divergent, as we shall see; yet Bandung gave rise to the Non-Aligned Movement (NAM), which has continued to meet periodically as the most influential expression of Third World aspirations and demands upon the wealthy nations. The Bandung AA Conference is still acknowledged as its inspiration and starting point.

Talk of Pan-Asianism and Pan-Africanism, as well as of the global solidarity of colonised peoples, had been heard sporadically for nearly 30 years before Bandung. But there had been little effective action to make anything significant of those aspirations. Even at Bandung, Pan-Asianism as such was overshadowed by other topics.

The Cold War was at its height in 1954–5 when the idea of holding an AA conference took hold. The Korean War, the Taiwan Straits crisis and Vietnam's armed struggle for independence were all sources of tension and anxiety, along with nuclear testing in the Pacific and the

Captain Tack, an emissary of the Dutch VOC in 1686, is portrayed as an ogre in traditional Indonesian shadow puppet theatre.

Vasco da Gama
(1469–1524), the
Portuguese explorer.

THE END OF THE 'VASCO DA GAMA EPOCH'

Western colonial rule in Asia began with the establishment there of Portuguese, Spanish, Dutch, British and French naval power and commercial empires in the centuries after 1500, culminating in the mighty British Empire in India and elsewhere in the 19th century. (America followed suit in the Philippines between 1898 and 1946, and Japan in China, Korea and her 'Greater East Asia Co-Prosperity Sphere' between 1895 and 1945.) Despite wide differences in the durations and characters of those colonial empires, it was rightly observed by the Indian diplomat, K.M. Panikkar, in his widely-acclaimed book *Asia and Western Dominance*, that:

The four hundred and fifty years which began with the arrival of Vasco da Gama in Calicut (in 1498), and ended with the withdrawal of British forces from India in 1947 and of the European navies from China in 1949, constitute a clearly marked epoch in history… In spite of [various] changes and developments…the Vasco da Gama epoch presents a singular unity in its fundamental aspects. These may be stated as the dominance of maritime power over the land masses of Asia; the imposition of a commercial economy over communities whose economic life had not been based on international trade…and the domination of the peoples of Europe, who held the mastery of the sea, over the affairs of Asia.

While Panikkar was broadly right about the dates for the ending of Western dominance, European colonies continued to exist in parts of Asia and most of Africa until well after his book appeared. Algeria's independence was not fully achieved until 1962, Vietnam's in 1975, and Zimbabwe's in 1978. The white-ruled apartheid regime in South Africa persisted until 1990.

The end of the Vasco da Gama epoch was brought about by the Japanese onslaught on Pearl Harbour, the Philippines, Malaya-Singapore, the Dutch East Indies and Burma in 1941–2, which shattered irrevocably the moral authority of white colonial rulers and made the restoration of the Western colonial empires after World War II impossibly difficult. (The ending of British mastery of the seas after 1918 and the fratricidal nature of the two 'European civil wars' of the early 20th century had also paved the way towards that.) Asian nationalism and anti-colonial sentiment, which had already been stirring for many years in India, Burma, Indonesia, Vietnam and the Philippines, were enormously enhanced by the Japanese victories and the collapse of European naval power in the Pacific and Indian oceans. (But US naval power became even more dominant in both oceans during the decades after 1945, with US economic, cultural and 'neocolonial' influence over the whole of Asia growing to be almost as pervasive as European colonial rule had ever been.) Both Panikkar's book and the Bandung conference served at that time to highlight the historical transformation that had occurred and the complex Asian nationalist responses to the end of the epoch of direct colonial rule.

PAN-ASIANISM AND PAN-AFRICANISM: SOME PRECURSORS

A Congress of Oppressed Nationalities held at Brussels in February 1927 was attended by 175 delegates from organisations in 37 countries, including Nehru, Mohammed Hatta and other leading Asian and African nationalists. It gave rise to the League Against Imperialism, a Moscow-sponsored body whose patrons (initially) included such diverse luminaries as Einstein, George Lansbury, Madame Sun Yat-sen, Upton Sinclair and (dubiously) Romain Rolland. It had been preceded six months earlier by a smaller International Conference for Peace at Bierville—also in Belgium: there were few other places in Europe where such meetings were permissible—with representatives from India, the Netherlands Indies, China, Egypt and Senegal. A declaration was issued that 'Asia must have its rightful place in the consideration of world problems'.

Both meetings were strongly influenced by Lenin's analysis of imperialism (with the export of capital as 'its taproot') and by the Communist International in Moscow. Nehru gave a passionate address on 'India's exploitation—how India is maltreated, oppressed and plundered'. He described the Brussels conference and the League Against Imperialism in his report to the All-India Congress Committee as 'an event of first-class importance and likely to have far-reaching results'. In that he was to be disappointed. Little came of it in the troubled 1930s and World War II made any thought of further such gatherings impossible.

For Nehru, the Bandung meeting nearly 30 years later was 'the fulfilment of a dream—Asia reborn, proud and free, playing an important role in the community. At Brussels, this goal was proclaimed by a handful of nationalist leaders. At Bandung, it was realised…by spokesmen for well over a billion people'.

Pan-African congresses were also held in the 1920s, but were riven by the rivalry between Dr William de Bois and Marcus Garvey. A Pan-African Congress in New York in 1927 attracted African students in Europe, including Jomo Kenyatta of Kenya, but it too lost momentum in the 1930s.

A fifth congress in Manchester in 1945 was considered important, but the various African nationalist movements went their own ways essentially over the next decade or more until the Accra Conference of 1958 and the creation of the Organisation of African Unity, made up of independent governments in 1963.

Not long before India became independent in 1947, an unofficial Asian Relations Conference was held in New Delhi at the Red Fort (by which it became known) under the auspices of the Indian Council of World Affairs, which further advanced the idea of Asian solidarity. In January 1949, India also organised an Asian Relations Conference at government level (which included the Australian government, significantly) to decide on joint action to counter the Dutch 'second police action'—actually a full-scale military assault—against the struggling Republic of Indonesia. It produced results in the UN and within the US Congress, putting political and economic pressure on the Dutch, which was a major factor in the Dutch decision some time later to abandon its military strategy and resume negotiation with the Republic, leading to the granting of independence to Indonesia in December 1949.

In the 18th–century Javanese courts, tigers were set to fight buffaloes; these contests were considered a metaphor for the relations between the Dutch VOC (the tiger, being quicker but with less stamina) and the Javanese themselves (the slow but powerful buffalo).

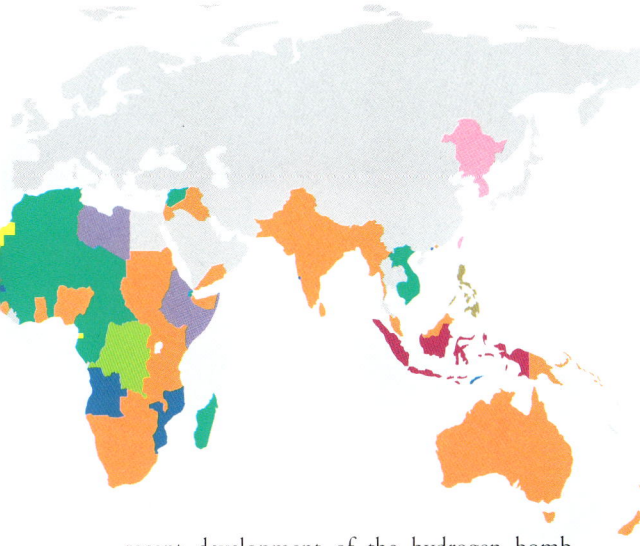

THE COLONIAL WORLD IN 1939

Colonies, protectorates, dominions and League of Nations trusteeships in Africa, Asia and the Pacific in the year 1939.

BRITISH
- Ascension
- St Helena
- Tristan da Cunha
- Gold Coast
- Nigeria
- Northern and Southern Rhodesia
- South Africa
- Basutoland
- Swaziland
- Bechuanaland
- South-West Africa
- British Somaliland
- Tanganyika
- Zanzibar
- Nyasaland
- Uganda
- Sudan
- Egypt
- Prince Edward Islands
- Mauritius
- Seychelles
- Socotra
- British Indian Ocean Territory
- Laccadives
- South Arabian Protectorate
- Iraq
- Transjordan
- India
- Burma
- Ceylon
- Andaman Islands
- Nicobar Islands
- Chagos Archipelago
- Cocos (Keeling) Islands
- Christmas Island
- Malaya
- North Borneo
- Singapore
- Hong Kong
- Australia
- New Zealand
- Papua New Guinea
- Gilbert Islands
- Nauru
- Fiji
- Kermadec Islands
- Santa Cruz Islands
- Solomon Islands
- Bismarck Archipelago
- New Hebrides
- Gambia
- Sierra Leone
- Kenya

FRENCH
- Morocco
- Algeria
- Tunisia
- Lebanon
- Syria
- French West Africa
- French Equatorial Africa
- Djibouti
- Madagascar
- Réunion
- Îles Crozet
- Îles Saint-Paul
- Îles Amsterdam
- Îles Loyauté
- New Caledonia
- New Hebrides
- Laos
- Cambodia
- Vietnam
- French Somaliland

DUTCH
- Netherlands East Indies

BELGIAN
- Belgian Congo
- Burundi
- Rwanda

PORTUGUESE
- Timor
- São Tomé and Príncipe
- Angola
- Mozambique
- Goa
- Macau
- Portuguese Guinea

SPANISH
- Spanish Guinea
- Canary Islands
- Spanish Sahara
- Spanish South Morocco

ITALIAN
- Libya
- Italian East Africa

AMERICAN
- The Philippines
- Palau
- Guam
- Mariana Islands
- Marshall Islands
- Wake Island

JAPANESE
- Korea
- Manchukuo (Inner Manchuria)
- Taiwan
- Ryukyu Islands
- Ogasawara Islands

recent development of the hydrogen bomb.

Talk of neutralism, non-alignment or the creation of a 'Third Force' to offset the two great power blocs was much in the air, especially in India, Burma and Indonesia, but the concept of non-alignment as a political force was still rudimentary. Yet the idea gained much wider acceptance in the years after Bandung, giving rise to a Conference of Non-Aligned Nations at Belgrade in 1961, from which arose the NAM. It has continued to exist until today, despite various ups and downs and disputes about just what non-alignment meant in changing circumstances.

Behind the debates that occurred at Bandung between the US-aligned group of strongly anti-communist countries and the smaller non-aligned group, as well as the dramas over China's attendance there as a member of the communist camp, we can discern a more subtle, muted contest between two other radically different world-views: that of John Foster Dulles on the one hand and Nehru on the other. The former's approach to a world seen as sharply polarised into two camps was upheld by the pro-Western members of Dulles's network of collective security treaties in East Asia (SEATO), the Middle East (CENTO) and Europe (NATO), who

THE RISE AND FALL OF THE COLONIAL EMPIRES

Portugal and Spain had created the first of the European colonial empires in the 16th century, the former in India and eastern Asia, the latter in the Americas (and later the Philippines). Portugal's remarkable maritime empire consisted of a network of trading posts seeking pepper and spices (and converts to Christianity) across much of Africa and Asia—most notably at Calicut, Goa, Malacca (the richest of the spice trading centres), Macau and Timor—as well as in Brazil.

Spain built up the largest of the early empires in Central and South America, largely on the basis of gold, plunder and slaves, but failed to make good use of it (the Netherlands got much of the ultimate commercial benefit from it) and lost nearly all of it by the early 19th century. But she later picked up some small colonies along the northern African coast during the late-19th-century 'grab for Africa'.

Ships and traders of the Dutch East India Company (the Verenigde Oostindische Compagnie) pursued the Portuguese and harassed them in the East Indies throughout the 17th century, establishing the basis of their East Indies colonial empire at Batavia (now Jakarta) in 1619 and the Spice Islands, seizing Malacca from the Portuguese in 1642, and later also Ceylon and Cape of Good Hope (South Africa). But the VOC initially sought only to establish a network of trading posts, without wanting to extend territorial control over wider areas—a costly business— or to establish colonies of European settlers there. Only in the 19th century, after coffee, sugar and other

A Dutch map of the Indonesian archipelago first published in 1598.

plantation crops became lucrative, did they extend direct control over Java and later the Outer Islands of what is now Indonesia. Monopolies of trade in lucrative commodities like pepper and spices were initially their main concerns. They had reduced the Portuguese to the status of a relatively minor colonial power by the 18th century.

A Portuguese-speaking mestizo his wife in 17th-century Indones

The British and French were latecomers in the competition for colonies, only becoming major players in the mid-18th century in India and North America, where colonies of European settlers were established on the northeastern seaboard and in Canada in the 17th century. Wars between them in the 18th century resulted in the French losing in Canada to the British and being gradually squeezed out of India (except for the tiny enclave of Pondicherry), which reduced France to a minor role as a colonial power. Napoleon tried to remedy that through the seizure of Egypt in the 1790s. Dreams of following in the footsteps of Alexander the Great (400 BCE) towards India kept French colonial ambitions alive, as did numerous French expeditions sent across the world in the hope, partly, of finding new lands to conquer and maintain 'la gloire'. They briefly held the Netherlands Indies and the Cape of Good Hope during the Napoleonic Wars. Later they seized a foothold in Vietnam in the hope of opening up a river route into southern China where lucrative markets were thought (wrongly) to await them. Vietnam later proved to be a costly nemesis for them, as also did the colonies they seized in northern Africa during the 'grab for Africa' years towards the end of the 19th century.

Britain built up the greatest of the colonial empires in the 19th century on the basis of her dominant sea power—after the Battle of Trafalgar in 1805 enabled her to 'rule the waves' for roughly a century—and her lead in the Industrial Revolution. Both factors gave her a dominant position in world trade until World War I. India was for her the 'jewel in the crown of empire', the largest and richest of her colonies. It has been said that the empire was acquired 'in a fit of absence of mind'. That is too colourful a phrase, but there were voices opposing colonial expansion as well as adventurers and those with vested interests advocating it in London after the loss of the American colonies in the war of American independence of 1776–83. The establishment of control over Canada, much of India, Australia, New Zealand and later South Africa was not very controversial at home and followed naturally from the extension of Britain's naval power and commercial hegemony in the 19th century. Other colonies in Africa, Malaya-Singapore, the Pacific Islands and elsewhere were more problematic—and very costly, in many cases.

But Britain had one unique advantage in that it had a strong anti-colonial lobby, deriving from her unhappy American experience (and later Canadian demands for self-government), which meant that even the maintenance of colonial rule over India was hotly debated and generally seen (though not by Winston Churchill) as not a permanent regime but essentially a step towards ultimate self-government and eventual independence. The white settler 'dominions' of Canada, Australia, New Zealand and South Africa had gradually become self-governing over the course of a century before World War II. Debates on Indian

The port city of Banten in West Java, where first the Portuguese then later the Dutch established fortified trading posts.

independence developed strongly in the 20 years before 1941 and the decision by the Labour government to concede independence to her in 1946–7, then in due course to other British colonies as well, was widely supported as a sensible and progressive measure. In that respect Britain was luckier than others in her experience of colonial rule.

The US had only a brief phase as a colonial power, mainly in the Philippines between 1898 and 1946, plus a few small islands in the Caribbean. But she had always had a strong anti-colonial lobby, with domestic sugar planters opposed to allowing Philippines sugar into the home market and therefore favouring an early grant of independence. In 1935, legislation was enacted to concede independence there after a 'commonwealth' stage of 10 years, which was interrupted by the Pacific War, but only by one year. In 1946, on 4 July, symbolically, the Philippines became the first of the Western colonies to achieve independence, although still closely bound to the US in various ways.

Japan aspired to acquire colonies or semi-colonial 'spheres of influence' in Korea and China when she saw how vigorously the Europeans were striving for them. She succeeded in Taiwan, Korea, parts of northern China and some central Pacific islands, in the form of a League of Nations mandate. Her bid to expand that empire in 1941–5 was crucial to the ending of colonial rule throughout Asia.

were at times almost as averse to Nehru's notions of non-alignment and a 'third way' as to the communist bloc itself. Nehru's approach embodied a still rudimentary doctrine of non-alignment, deriving as much from a wish to avoid dependence on any outside power or bloc as from his wish to 'widen the area of peace' in a world of dangerous international tensions. Indonesia's independent 'free and active' foreign policy or Burma's vaguely Buddhist advocacy of non-aggression were similar in spirit but less clearly formulated.

Twenty-nine nations were represented at Bandung, all except seven or eight of them newly independent (depending on definitions), most of them strongly imbued with a spirit of nationalism. Only six of them were African—Egypt, Sudan, Ethiopia, the Gold Coast (soon to become Ghana), Libya and Liberia. Only 25 Asian or African nations were yet members of the United Nations. (The People's Republic of China was not yet one of them, since Taiwan still held that seat, with dogged US backing.) By 1965, that number had risen to 53, and by 1975, to 76, with China now a member and Taiwan out. How much influence the Bandung conference exerted on the course of events that brought about that sweeping transformation is arguable, but it certainly contributed greatly to the climate of world opinion in which this transformation became possible.

How much more than 'mere symbolism' and ardent nationalism, however, did Bandung represent? Some would say 'a great deal', but others not much beyond 'words, words, words'. Which view comes closest to the truth? That is a question we must return to later.

1955 and 2005: Some contrasts

The Bandung conference can best be seen today as a fleeting moment of convergence of various trends in the postcolonial history of the world. It produced a high water mark of dedication to noble ideals, high hopes

RELIGIONS AT BANDUNG

Little was heard from or about the world's great religions in the course of the AA Conference, despite the fact that they originated in Asian countries. All had devotees there of various stripes, except Judaism, Zoroastrianism, Taoism and Confucianism (if the latter can be classed as a religion; and in any case, Zhou Enlai acknowledged explicitly that he was an atheist—probably the only delegate to do so); but neither Islam, Buddhism nor Christianity were mentioned much except in the odd quotation.

Nearly half the countries represented there had predominantly Muslim populations and were represented by at least nominal Muslim leaders, who all trooped off to the mosque for their Friday prayers. But the principal bond between them seemed to be opposition to Israel and support for Palestine's cause (and hatred of Zionism, in some cases) rather than advancement of their faith. The Middle Eastern countries came across as more Arab and nationalist than Islamic. Pakistan, the most avowedly Muslim state, was little different from the others in that respect.

Some of the delegates from the six mainly Buddhist countries did project a distinctly Buddhist

Laos entirely approves of the Five Principles [of the Panch Shila]... And we cannot fail to remark how this perspective, by the moral attitude which it implies, corresponds with our Buddhist teachings.
– Katay Don Sasorith, Laotian delegate

character, especially U Nu. (But not the almost British-style Sir John Kotelawala!) Sayings of the Buddha cropped up in their speeches more than the sayings of Mohammed or Christ in any others.

Of the two specifically Christian countries, Ethiopia and the Philippines, only the former's delegate touched upon the country's religion. The voluble Carlos Romulo had a lot to say on most topics, but nothing to say on Christianity.

If there were missionaries there, of any faith, they did not make much of an impact. (Yet what a marvellous opportunity it must have been for them!)

Bandung was surrounded, as it happened, by well-armed Darul Islam rebels against their 'infidel' government in Jakarta, the organiser of the conference. Outside the city, and along the road from Bogor to Bandung, it was often unsafe to travel at dusk. In India, Nehru had survived an assassination attempt by a Hindu extremist only a month previously. Religion does not always go hand in hand with peace.

Most of the Middle Eastern delegates seemed to fit the mould of the secularising Muslim society that Kemal Ataturk had tried to create in Turkey, especially Nasser. (He had not long since banned the Muslim Brotherhood in Egypt after it stirred up riots against him.) For them, nationalism and ideology bulked larger than religion as the driving force of the new Asia and Africa.

The Laotian prime minister and delegate to the Bandung conference, Katay Don Sasorith, in Buddhist dress.

BANDUNG...'THE COOLEST AND NICEST SPOT IN JAVA'

Bandung had several advantages over any other city in Indonesia as the site for a big international conference—a mild climate, suitable conference facilities and accommodation, easy access from Jakarta (about 3–4 hours by car or train; barely half an hour by plane) and a sophisticated social ambience. Moreover, as the headquarters of the renowned Siliwangi division, a major Army base, it could readily ensure security for the participants—an important consideration at a time when Darul Islam insurgents roamed freely in the surrounding mountains and forests. An Indian official remarked that

> Bandung provided the ideal surroundings for the conference. Situated some 2,400 feet above sea level amidst small hills and lovely valleys, neither too warm nor too cold, this little city, the pleasantest in Indonesia, seemed to spread welcome and a wholesome spirit of compromise. Two fine big buildings, renovated and redecorated for the occasion, provided excellent conference halls and rooms; one of them, 'the Concordia', was especially renamed Gedung Merdeka—the House of Freedom—which had a good psychological effect on the first big meeting of Asian and African people… All guests without exception had a good word to say about the well thought-out arrangements.

Bandung in the 1950s was a much smaller, less densely populated city than the crowded industrial centre it is today. The population was about 840,000.

(It has grown to nearly three times that size at present.) It still had a lot of the relaxed atmosphere of the late colonial era when it was essentially an administrative and recreational centre for Dutch planters from the flourishing tea and coffee estates in the nearby mountains.

Race relations between the Dutch, Eurasians and 'native' Indonesians were more relaxed and cordial there than anywhere else in Java, and remained so until well into the 1960s. It had earlier been the headquarters of the Dutch colonial army and later became a senior officers' training centre for the new Indonesian army. It had the country's only technologically oriented university, originally called the Technische Hogeschool (where Sukarno had studied for his degree in architecture in the 1920s), which later became the renowned Institut Teknologi Bandung (ITB), one of Indonesia's top universities and one of the town's architectural gems. Bandung was famous in the 1930s for its fine restaurants, shops and lively social life, with Jalan Braga regarded in those days as the smartest street in any Indonesian city. The main conference hall, Gedung Merdeka, was on the corner of Braga and Jalan Asia-Afrika, close to the Homann Hotel, where many of the delegates stayed.

Gedung Sate, a government office building.

Until late in the 19th century, the city itself was quite small, as Bandung and the surrounding area had not yet been developed as a major region of the Dutch plantation enterprise. While the upland Priangan area to the west had been a major centre of coffee cultivation for well over a century, coffee had not initially been a plantation crop but was produced by peasant farmers under heavy compulsion. Only after Dutch planters began to produce tea, coffee and rubber on large plantations after 1870 did Bandung itself start to grow steadily as a largely Dutch city.

Bandung was touted as 'the Paris of the East' in the 1920–30s, even called 'the Queen of Eastern Mountain Cities' and 'the coolest and nicest spot in Java' in a gushy tourist brochure put out by *Bandoeng Vooruit* (Forward Bandung). 'It lies at the bottom of a green cup that is surrounded by mountains and ringed with lovely little hill stations, some of them suburbs', such as Lembang and Ciumbuleuit. Hardly any Dutchmen lived on the other side of the main east-west road (of which Jalan Asia-Afrika is now the central part), in the much hotter, industrialising southern parts of the city, occupied mainly by Indonesians.

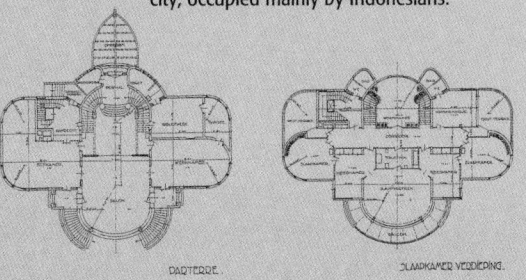

The floorplans (above) for Villa Isola, seen from a distance on the left.

There was talk around 1930 of making Bandung—rather than Batavia (Jakarta)—the capital of the Dutch colony. Some government agencies like the railways moved their main offices up there. It also had the Pasteur Institute and the vulcanology centre, which gave it an unusually high proportion of the colony's scientific and engineering expertise.

At the time of the AA Conference, Bandung had changed relatively little from the 1930s 'garden city' it had been, with some of the most interesting modern architecture to be found anywhere in the Dutch colony. Several unusually forward-looking Dutch architects, all adopting modernist principles of design, all associated with the Technische Hogeschool, had exerted a great influence on the physical appearance of the city over the previous decades. No other Indonesian city had developed such a distinctive—and distinctively modern—style of architecture until the 1980s. It was an architecture intended, of course, for the tastes and needs of the colonial masters, not for the local people. But it was also influenced by Indonesian building styles and traditions, notably in the Gedung Sate and the ITB.

These architects were seeking to create a 'New Indies style', combining modern European construction techniques with Indonesian elements—especially in such matters as air-flows and rooflines—of which those at ITB, Maclaine Pont's masterpiece, soon became the best known. Gerber had earlier designed the Gedung Sate with broadly similar aims in mind, with its pagoda-like central tower (reminiscent of a pointy *sate* stick to the locals). On the other hand, Villa Isola, designed by Schoemaker, was a strikingly modernist building in the northern hill suburbs of Bandung, which became a teachers college after independence. The forthrightly modernist-functionalist reconstruction by Aalbers in 1939 of the Grand Savoy Homann, close to the Gedung Merdeka, was his best-known work with its strong, curved lines, a 'modern liner style'.

Altogether, Bandung was a very interesting place, as well as a cool and beautiful one.

SUKARNO (1901–1970)

Bandung came to mean more to Sukarno* than to any other Asian leader, although he had only the limited role there of making the opening address. But his ideas, his phrases and much of his strongly anti-colonialist ideology suffused the entire atmosphere of the conference through the words and thoughts of other Indonesian participants—Ali Sastroamidjojo, Sunario, Roeslan Abdulgani, and the large Indonesian delegation. And over the next decade, he championed the 'Bandung spirit' and the need for a second AA Conference with more passion than anyone else.

Sukarno had suffered imprisonment at the hands of Indonesia's colonial rulers, the Dutch, for nearly as long as Nehru had at the hands of the British; and he enjoyed much the same status as the outstanding leader of his nation during its 1945–9 armed struggle for independence as well as for nearly 20 years before that—and also for 10 years after Bandung. He above all other Indonesians had upheld the banner of nationalism against both the Dutch and the Japanese (along with Mohammed Hatta, who proclaimed independence with him jointly in August 1945), at an often high personal cost.

In his political ideology, his anti-colonialism and his youthful flirtation with Marxism, he had many similarities with Nehru, although the two men were temperamentally very different and not at all close personally.

He was a superb orator and an intensely charismatic figure, an extrovert, a commanding presence, utterly self-confident, a born leader from his early student days until his overthrow in 1965–7. One of his biographers, J.D. Legge, has described him as

a highly individual leader with his own instinctive and mercurial style. His vanity, his charm, his political resourcefulness and his unpredictability were a source of admiration and exasperation to observers. Among his countrymen he inspired devotion or hostility, but never indifference… To some he was a dedicated leader—the real maker of Indonesia and the sustainer and preserver of the nation after independence. To others he was a disaster, a waster of the nation's resources in policies of domestic extravagance and foreign adventures, a man seduced by power… His intoxicating sense of the world in movement, and his philosophy of continuing revolution diverted attention from the immediate tasks of governing.

He was in many respects a visionary, the man who conjured up dreams of 'a golden bridge' to a

and also some shrewd politics among the newly independent nations of Asia and Africa. But that moment of convergence soon gave way to divergence, and to the disputes, recriminations and wars between them in the 1960s, as the world order became more fissured and multipolar.

Shall we ever see its like again? Or the realisation of those early hopes and aspirations? Such questions can no longer be asked of the generation of 1955, of course, but they will remain as a challenge for the generations of 2005 and after—our children and grandchildren and even theirs—to answer, in all parts of the world. But the Bandung origins of those early postcolonial aspirations towards Asian and African unity and solidarity, and of Sukarno's call 'to build the world anew', are still worth pondering in our very different ideological climate.

Sukarno at age 15 (left), and waving to crowds in 1957 (above).

and Indonesia's 1955 national elections (her first ever, and fairest until 2004), 'Let's bury the political parties'. He then proceeded between 1959 and 1966 to bring about his notion of a 'Guided Democracy'— under a presidential constitution—which became increasingly authoritarian.

In those years, he devoted an exorbitant amount of time and resources to foreign policy issues, to the neglect of domestic administration— most notably to the recovery of West Irian from the Dutch, and the semi-military *Konfrontasi* against Malaysia and the British military bases there. That was bound up with his radical reinterpretation of non-alignment by invoking the struggle between the 'New Emerging Forces' and the 'Old Established Forces'. This caused wrangles with Nehru, Nasser and others over the Non-Aligned Movement and a frantic push in 1964–5 for a second AA Conference, which proved a disastrous failure. In that, he probably did more harm than good, sadly, to the idea of AA unity that Bandung had tried to create.

future Indonesian 'just and prosperous society', dreams he used to inspire the diverse Indonesian peoples and unite them behind the banner of nationalism.

As a political leader, he was often a highly controversial figure, both at home and abroad. Chafing at the limitations of his mainly titular role as president within a Western parliamentary system, he proposed, not long after the Bandung conference

*Many Indonesians, including its first two presidents, have only one name. The forename Achmed was bestowed upon Sukarno in error by a Western journalist who felt he must have one, so he plucked it out of the air. It has been much repeated ever since.

Afro-Asian solidarity was a phrase to conjure with for some years after Bandung. Yet, within a decade, wars and disputes between the main Asian and African nations were making a mockery of the phrase. The Sino-Indian war of October 1962, the India–Pakistan dispute over Kashmir and a war between them in late 1965, coupled with the widening of the Sino-Soviet rift into intense rivalry throughout the 1960s, wreaked havoc not only with the ideal of AA unity but also with the very concept of non-alignment. What could it possibly mean now that the world was divided not just into two Cold War camps but several?

The attempt to hold a second AA Conference at Algiers in 1965 collapsed in acrimony and sharp divisions. No similar attempt has since been made—and in the current state of international politics it seems

unlikely that it ever will (although the celebration of the 50th anniversary of the conference may help to revive some of the original 'Bandung spirit').

Today, China, India and the 'Asian Tigers' have such fast-growing economies that predictions are heard in some quarters that several of them may surpass the West on global wealth tables by the middle of this century. On the other hand, much of Africa has become an economic disaster area, while the gap between the poor nations and the rich has widened exponentially. More than mere statements of goodwill and firm resolve to restore the spirit of Bandung unity will be needed if that trend

is to be reversed and the world made a better place again. Moreover, globalisation is blurring the sharp division of the world into two camps of rich and poor which gave rise to the NAM and the later notion of the Third World. Afro-Asian unity is a far less credible notion in such circumstances than it seemed to be in 1955.

Afro-Asian unity and solidarity could not be taken for granted either before the conference or after. It was conjured up with a great deal of effort (and some good luck and smart politics) as a by-product of the common urge to achieve consensus there. But the tense international situation of 1954–5 was also a key factor, to which we must now turn.

PARTICIPATING NATIONS AT THE BANDUNG CONFERENCE

A total of 30 nations were invited to the conference, of which the
29 nations listed below sent representatives.

THE FIVE SPONSORS
Burma
Ceylon
India
Indonesia
Pakistan

OTHER ASIAN
Afghanistan
Cambodia
China
Iran
Iraq
Japan
Jordan
Laos
Lebanon
Nepal
Philippines, the
Saudi Arabia
Syria
Thailand
Turkey
Vietnam, North
Vietnam, South
Yemen

AFRICAN
Egypt
Ethiopia
Gold Coast (later Ghana)
Liberia
Libya
Sudan

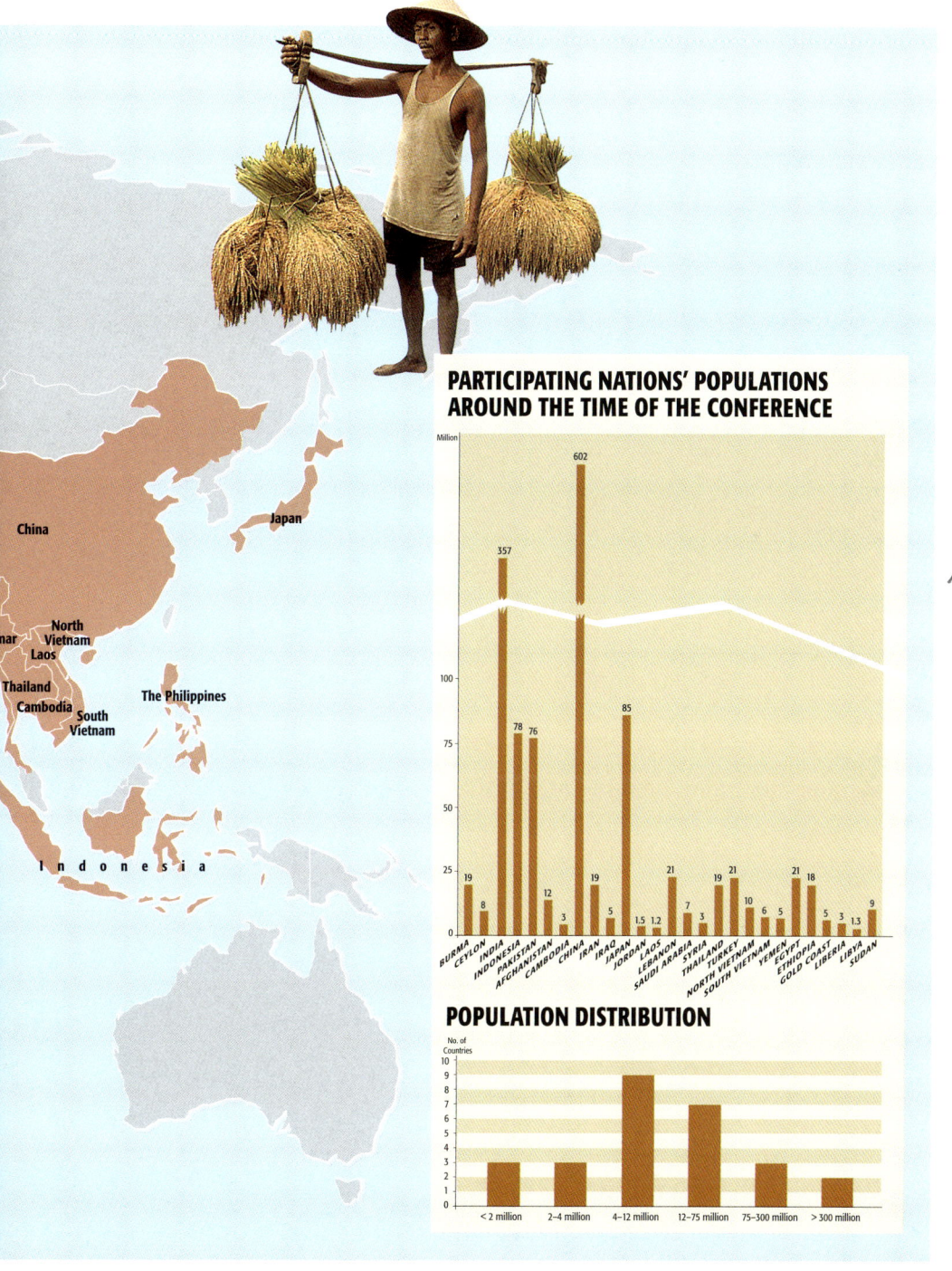

China

Japan

North
Vietnam
Laos

mar

Thailand
Cambodia
South
Vietnam

The Philippines

I n d o n e s i a

Australia

PARTICIPATING NATIONS' POPULATIONS AROUND THE TIME OF THE CONFERENCE

Million

602

357

100

85

78 76

75

50

25

19   19   21   19   21   21 18
8   12   5   7   10   6 5   5   9
3   1.5 1.2   3   3   1.3

0

BURMA · CEYLON · INDIA · INDONESIA · PAKISTAN · AFGHANISTAN · CAMBODIA · CHINA · IRAQ · JAPAN · JORDAN · LAOS · SAUDI ARABIA · LEBANON · SYRIA · THAILAND · TURKEY · NORTH VIETNAM · SOUTH VIETNAM · YEMEN · EGYPT · ETHIOPIA · GOLD COAST · LIBERIA · LIBYA · SUDAN

POPULATION DISTRIBUTION

No. of
Countries

10
9
8
7
6
5
4
3
2
1
0

| < 2 million | 2–4 million | 4–12 million | 12–75 million | 75–300 million | > 300 million |

TIMELINE: THE RISE AND FALL OF COLONIAL EMPIRES, 1400–1945

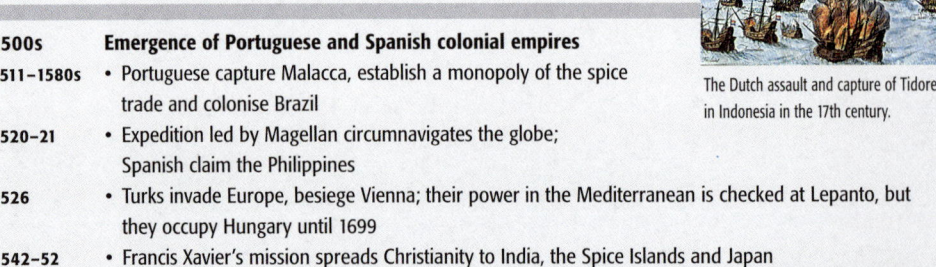

The Dutch assault and capture of Tidore fortress in Indonesia in the 17th century.

1400s	**Forerunners of Western colonial expansion**
1400–20	• Chinese voyages under Admiral Zheng He to Southeast Asia and Madagascar
1420–80	• Portuguese explorations of Africa's West Coast and the Indian Ocean
1492–4	• Columbus reaches America; beginnings of Spanish empire there
1498	• Portuguese reach India (Calicut); trading posts gradually built up across South and Southeast Asia

1500s	**Emergence of Portuguese and Spanish colonial empires**
1511–1580s	• Portuguese capture Malacca, establish a monopoly of the spice trade and colonise Brazil
1520–21	• Expedition led by Magellan circumnavigates the globe; Spanish claim the Philippines
1526	• Turks invade Europe, besiege Vienna; their power in the Mediterranean is checked at Lepanto, but they occupy Hungary until 1699
1542–52	• Francis Xavier's mission spreads Christianity to India, the Spice Islands and Japan

1600s	**Beginnings of Dutch, British and French colonies**
1602	• Dutch East India Company (VOC) builds up a trading empire in Java and the Spice Islands: Batavia (now Jakarta) becomes the centre of her colonial possessions
1605–1760	• British and French establish colonies in North America and factories in India
1622–1850s	• Japan is closed to foreigners by the Tokugawa Shogunate
1644	• China's Ming dynasty is overthrown by the Manchu; naval activity ceases
late 1600s	• Decline of India's Mughal dynasty

Aurangzeb, the last of the great Mughal emperors.

1700s	**French and British rivalry in North America and India**
early 1700s	• Portuguese and Spanish power wanes in Asia but continues in America
1750–1760s	• British power is much extended in India; French power is reduced there and in Canada
1755–1800	• Dutch VOC extends indirect rule (later direct rule) over Java
1776–83	• British lose North America, except Canada, in the American Revolution
1780–1790s	• British fail to open up trade links with China
1788	• Australia occupied by British (as a penal colony); French probing expeditions are excluded

1800s	**European colonial empires at their peak worldwide**
1800s	• Industrial Revolution in Britain and global naval supremacy give her commercial supremacy and enable colonial expansion worldwide
1807–11	• French take over Dutch colonies in Napoleonic era; Egypt occupied briefly
1811–16	• Raffles rules Java, founds Singapore; British gain Cape of Good Hope and Ceylon
1840–60	• China forced to open her ports to foreign trade; opium trade expands
1850s	• Japan forced by Perry to open herself to foreign trade; Meiji regime replaces Shogunate, then modernises and later industrialises Japan rapidly

1857	• 'Indian Mutiny' crushed: British control of India tightened
1862–87	• French colonies in Indochina are established, others in Africa follow soon after
1885	• Indian National Congress founded, germ of strongest Asian nationalist movement
1890s	• Jose Rizal, pioneering nationalist leader in the Philippines' resistance to Spain, is shot by firing squad as 'the first Asian martyr to independence'; 'Grab for Africa'; US seizes the Philippines; Japan seizes Taiwan (and later Korea); Dutch extend control across Indonesia; the ideology of Imperialism is 'at high tide'

1900s	**Nationalist resistance to colonialism develops; decolonisation after 1945**
1900	• Boxer Rebellion in China; European forces sack Beijing
1904–5	• Russo-Japanese War: Japanese victory at Tsushima inspires Asian nationalists
1912	• China's Manchu dynasty overthrown, Sun Yat-sen establishes Republic of China, displaced soon after by military warlords and civil war; Chiang Kai-shek emerges; Chinese Communist Party established
1914–18	• World War I ('The First European Civil War'); Woodrow Wilson's Fourteen Points raise hopes of colonial liberation (but are frustrated); League of Nations established to maintain peace (but fails); Fascist regimes established in Italy and Germany

Japanese soldiers and the military flag.

1920s	• Gandhi leads anti-colonial resistance in India; Nehru joins him in Congress Party leadership; negotiations with the British over independence become deadlocked
1927	• Brussels Congress of 'League against Imperialism, Colonial Oppression and for National Independence'
1927–30	• Sukarno unites Indonesian nationalist movement, but is firmly suppressed by the Dutch
1931	• Japan invades Manchuria
1937	• 'Rape of Nanking' and Sino-Japanese War (the beginning of the 'Pacific War')
1939–45	• World War II ('The Second European Civil War')
1941	• Attack on Pearl Harbour greatly extends Pacific War as Japan seizes US, British and Dutch colonies in eastern Asia, occupies French colonies; colonial authorities undermined terminally; invasion of India threatened; 'Asia for the Asians' and 'Japanese Co-Prosperity Sphere' slogans intensify anti-colonial and nationalist sentiment and determination to resist return of colonial rulers
1945	• Defeat of Germany in April and Japan in August ends World War II

The bombing of Pearl Harbour by the Japanese and the sinking of the *USS Arizona*.

THE INTERNATIONAL BACKGROUND:
COLD WAR, DECOLONISATION, VIETNAM, CHINA-US TENSIONS

When the idea of an Afro-Asian conference began to take shape in 1954, the Cold War was at its height, in real danger of becoming a nuclear hot war. And the flashpoints which gave rise to the most alarming fears of that were all in Asia, all adjacent to China and all dangerously threatening to her: Korea, Vietnam and the Taiwan Straits. (Also not far away were US nuclear weapon testing grounds in the Pacific, at Bikini Atoll and Eniwetok in the Marshall Islands, the scenes of atomic bomb tests and the first devastating hydrogen bomb test.) Yet, Asians had little or no voice in the decision-making relevant to those perilous developments, a fact that was increasingly resented in the euphoric aftermath of their recent achievement of independence.

While a mandarin gestures in alarm, Queen Victoria (England), Kaiser Wilhelm II (Germany), Tsar Nicholas II (Russia), Marianne (France) and a samurai (Japan) vie for a piece of the pie (*Chine* is French for 'China').

The key decisions which would sway the course of events in Asia towards war or peace were being made not in Asian capitals—except to some extent in Beijing (reactively)—but still in Washington, London, Moscow and Paris, the capitals of the nuclear powers (or others trying urgently to join them). So also were the decisions about the fate of the few remaining colonies in Asia—French Indochina, British Malaya and Singapore, as well as the sleepy Portuguese relics of Goa, Macau and Timor—and the large number of them in Africa, where the process of decolonisation, generated throughout Asia by Japan's overthrow of the Western colonial empires during World War II, had so far only just begun. Liberation struggles were still in their infancy in Africa.

Bringing an end to colonial rule across the world—and what Sukarno called 'neocolonialism and imperialism', which he saw as colonialism's later face—was as important a goal of the Bandung conference as reducing the dangers of the Cold War. But the two issues were dangerously entangled in the case of Vietnam.

Another important objective at Bandung, at least in the eyes of Nehru and U Nu, Burma's prime minister, was to bring an end to the non-recognition, international isolation and demonisation of the communist People's Republic of China (PRC) by the US and its allies, and to reverse her exclusion from the seat allotted to China in 1945 as one of the permanent members of the UN Security Council. The refusal of the US to recognise Mao Zedong's communist regime and its continued recognition of the discredited Kuomintang (KMT) regime of Chiang Kai-shek in Taiwan as the official government of China caused outrage in many Asian countries who were not bound up in the rigid imperatives of the Cold War and had their own good reasons to want to see China playing an active part in the comity of Asian nations and the UN. The decision of the US to interpose its Seventh Fleet in the Straits of Taiwan to deter any Chinese attempt to invade Taiwan also worried them as a potential (and very provocative) trigger to a nuclear Third World War.

An anti-US PRC propaganda poster, 'The Night of Celebration' (above), with Mao Zedong depicted centrally; Chiang Kai-shek (1887–1975), leader of the KMT (below).

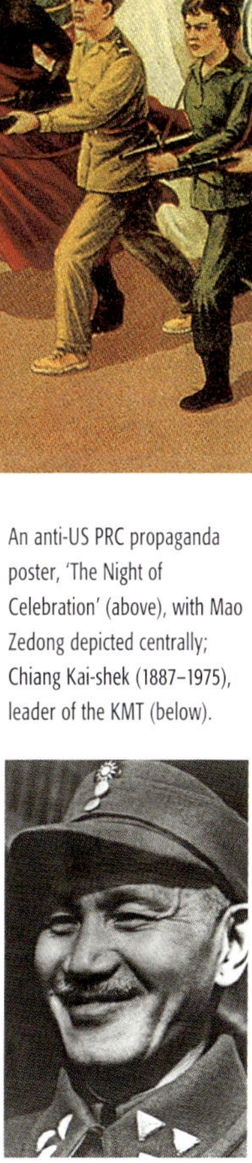

Colonialism and decolonisation

One reason why the issue of colonialism bulked so large at Bandung was that the progress made in the late 1950s towards granting independence to former colonies in Asia seemed to have stalled, largely under the pressures of the Cold War. No colonies obtained their independence between 1949 and 1954 except the special cases of Libya (formerly under Italy, but taken over by Britain 10 years earlier), and the British protectorates, Egypt and Sudan. The French were showing no sign of conceding more than a nominal degree of sovereignty to their three 'Associated States' in Indochina—Vietnam, Laos and Cambodia—and were relying on sheer military force rather than political concessions to counter the nationalist appeal of Ho Chi Minh and his Vietminh regime based mainly in the rural areas of northern Vietnam. Nor were they taking any serious steps towards liberating their North African colonies—Morocco, Tunisia or Algeria. Meanwhile, the British were relying primarily on military force to suppress the communist-led

An artist's impression of the Battle of Isandlwana, a pyrrhic victory for the Zulu nation against the British colonisers during the Anglo-Zulu war of the late 19th century.

FRANCE AND HER COLONIES

The French colonies in Indochina and North Africa, which caused so many problems for her and many others in the postwar years, had nearly all been acquired relatively late in the colonial era, mostly after 1870, well after France had lost her first colonial empire in the middle of the 18th century. They must all have cost the country far more, overall, than they ever yielded financially. So the reasons why they were thought to matter so greatly and why France lagged so far behind the US, Britain and Holland in ceding independence to them, are tangled and puzzling questions.

Several elements that form part of the answer can be suggested. Colonies were widely sought after in the later 19th century as a sign—and indeed, an essential condition—of national greatness. (This was shown to be a fallacy by the Dutch experience of more rapid economic progress without the financial burden of an colony to sustain). 'La gloire' comes into the picture, a symbol of France's earlier greatness. The belief that the French concept of 'assimilation' of subject races to the higher level of civilisation represented by the French language, culture and citizenship made available to them was superior to the more mundane British and Dutch approaches to the 'mission civilisatrice' seems to have also played a part in at least some intellectual circles. The mystique, romanticism and exoticism associated with the Foreign Legion (of central

importance to the military control of their empire) probably also had something to do with it.

On a more mundane level, the domestic politics of the many French colons residing in Algeria who were resistant to concessions that might serve as a precedent for granting independence to France's colonies, along with the international politics of reluctance to be pushed around by the British or Americans, undoubtedly had a big psychological effect in making the French loathe to part with their colonies. President de Gaulle's abrupt (and courageous) decision to cede independence to Algeria in 1962, after seven years of a brutal colonial war there, was made in the face of great political difficulties.

COLONY	ACQUIRED	LOST OR INDEPENDENCE CEDED
North America	1640s–1700	1759–1803
Indian colonies	1650s–1700	1750–1790s
Vietnam	1830	1949–54
Cambodia	1863–5	1949–54
Laos (protectorate)	1893	1949–54
Algeria	1830	1962
Morocco (protectorate)	1912	1956
Tunisia (protectorate)	1881	1956
Other African colonies	1840–1910	1960–70s

insurgency in Malaya, called 'The Emergency', and the Mau-Mau revolt in Kenya. They showed little inclination to move towards independence in either case. Elsewhere in Africa, the prospects of eventual freedom from colonial rule still looked infinitely remote.

The political dynamics behind the decolonisation process and the Cold War were not directly connected, although there were close linkages between them at times, especially during the climax of the French Indochina War in Vietnam in 1953–4. Strangely enough, one of the strongest impulses towards the wave of demands for decolonisation that swept across Asia after 1945 had derived from US

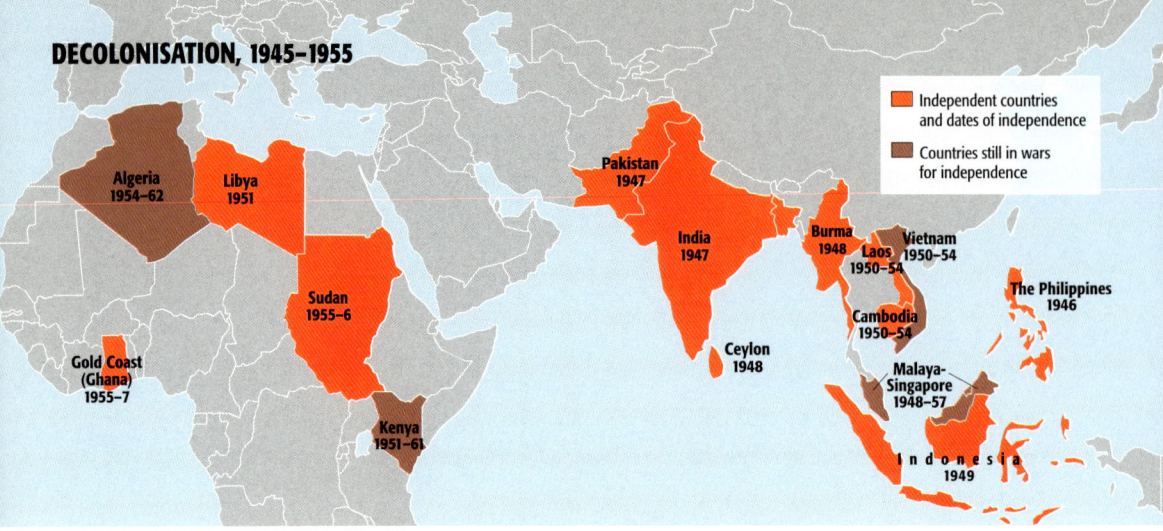

DECOLONISATION, 1945–1955

Independent countries and dates of independence

Countries still in wars for independence

Algeria 1954–62
Libya 1951
Pakistan 1947
India 1947
Burma 1948
Laos 1950–54
Vietnam 1950–54
The Philippines 1946
Sudan 1955–6
Cambodia 1950–54
Ceylon 1948
Gold Coast (Ghana) 1955–7
Malaya-Singapore 1948–57
Kenya 1951–61
Indonesia 1949

President Roosevelt's disdain for the French and British colonial empires, most strikingly expressed in the 'Four Freedoms' of the 1941 Atlantic Charter and later in the United Nations charter of 1945, all of which gave great encouragement to the independence movements of India, Indonesia, Vietnam and elsewhere—but great dismay to the colonial powers and their lackeys everywhere. Yet, it was the crisis point of the French colonial war to retain control of the colony, coupled with the strategic implications of Vietnam's proximity to China, that had the most immediate bearing upon the course of events which led to the Bandung conference.

Why were the newly independent nations so concerned to maintain support for the anti-colonialist struggles of their still oppressed comrades elsewhere in the world in 1955? They had no very strong motivations to do so by way of national interest of a strategic or commercial nature. But ideologically, they were strongly in sympathy, as much of the rhetoric of Bandung revealed. And at a time of intense ideological conflict worldwide between the communist bloc and the capitalist 'Free World', many of the newly independent nations of Asia were reluctant to become closely aligned in any way with either camp, particularly the one that was still oppressing freedom fighters seeking independence. Another major impulse towards their hatred of colonial rule had derived from the utter failure of the Western colonial regimes to provide any worthwhile defence for their colonies against the Japanese onslaught in 1941–2, which shattered the old myths of white superiority that had been an essential pillar of colonial authority.

Sturm über Asien... *irresistible forces... hurricanes of national awakening...*
– Sukarno, opening speech

One of the most important factors contributing to the global push towards the ending of colonialism had been the granting of independence to India (hence also Pakistan, and later to Ceylon and Burma) by a Labour Party government in Britain in 1946–8, after several decades of debate about the matter. That represented a decisive step towards the dismantling of colonial rule more widely, for if the greatest of the imperial powers felt it had to concede independence to its largest and most valuable colony, the psychological effects elsewhere were bound to be far-reaching. Even France under the imperious President Charles de Gaulle eventually had to accept that politically unpalatable fact in Algeria. Yet neither the French, the Portuguese, the Spanish nor even the Dutch were initially prepared to accept the inevitable. Belief in their '*mission civilisatrice*' remained too strong there. It was something Bandung still had to counter. And perhaps it did, since a great wave of decolonisation occurred in the early 1960s, due as much to the new zeitgeist created in part by Bandung as to anything else, or as the British prime minister, Harold Macmillan, put it in 1960, to the 'winds of change' sweeping the world.

The Battle of Dien Bien Phu and the Vietnam Crisis

The most bitterly fought and potentially dangerous struggle for independence in Asia in the early 1950s took place in Vietnam, where the communist (and also intensely nationalist) Vietminh, led by Ho Chi Minh, based mainly in impregnable rural hideouts or in the mountainous parts of northern Vietnam, were successfully defying French efforts to reassert military control over their colony. The conflict had become especially perilous because French and US approaches to the long and indecisive colonial war there were becoming radically divergent just as the military situation grew increasingly precarious for the French. The new Eisenhower regime, and in particular the crusty, truculent secretary

General Henri Navarre (1898–1983).

Vietminh territory

Under Vietminh control

Under French control

Map showing areas of Vietminh and French control in 1953, as well as the 1954 Partition Line.

of state, John Foster Dulles, was determined to curb any further extension of communist power in Asia lest it result in a 'domino effect' spreading across the whole of Southeast Asia.

But the French public was beginning to tire of its seemingly endless war against the Vietminh guerrilla forces. By 1953, talk of political negotiations to end the war was much in the air in Paris, with the shaky Laniel government quietly considering that negotiations towards a peace settlement with Ho Chi Minh might be unavoidable. (At about the same time, the Eisenhower administration was negotiating a ceasefire with the communist regime in Korea.) But France hoped it could first win a sufficiently impressive victory to be able to bargain from a position of strength, not weakness, towards some sort of partition between a communist North and a French-oriented South. A new military commander, General Navarre, was sent to Saigon with ambiguous instructions about the strategy he should pursue towards that end, which he chose to interpret in his own way in the much-vaunted 'Navarre Plan' to end the war. His aim was to force the Vietminh into a conventional, main-force battle in which superior French arms, tanks, air power and technology would bring them victory over the ragged guerrilla units of General Giap, the Vietminh commander.

To this end, Navarre made the fateful decision in November 1953 to build up a major French fortress around the remote interior hill

PHAM VAN DONG (1906–2000)

Born of a family of high-ranking mandarins, he was one of the founders of the Vietminh (Front for National Independence) with Ho Chi Minh in 1941, and remained one of Ho's closest associates. He took part in revolutionary activities in his youth, was arrested by the French in 1929 and was imprisoned on Poulo-Condore island till 1936. He held various government posts after 1945, among them Minister for Foreign Affairs and head of the North Vietnam delegation to the Geneva Conference of 1954 and the Bandung conference of 1955. He retained positions as prime minister and foreign minister into the 1960s.

A pontoon bridge used by the Vietminh to transport supplies to Dien Bien Phu (top); the French forces used trenches to survive artillery bombardment by the Vietminh (centre); General Giap, commander of the Vietminh forces, inspecting troops (right).

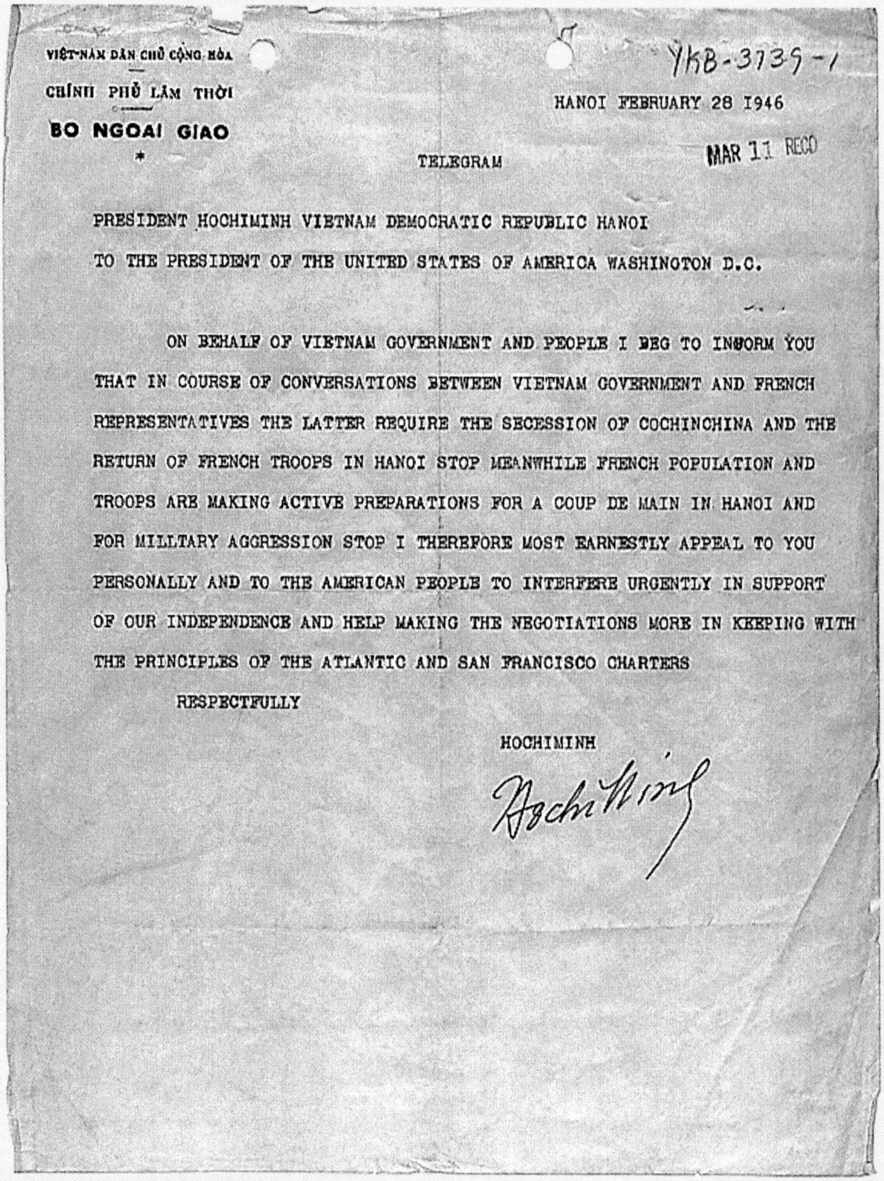

VIỆT-NAM DÂN CHỦ CỘNG HÒA

CHÍNH PHỦ LÂM THỜI

BO NGOAI GIAO

*

YKB-3739-1

HANOI FEBRUARY 28 1946

MAR 11 RECD

TELEGRAM

PRESIDENT HOCHIMINH VIETNAM DEMOCRATIC REPUBLIC HANOI

TO THE PRESIDENT OF THE UNITED STATES OF AMERICA WASHINGTON D.C.

ON BEHALF OF VIETNAM GOVERNMENT AND PEOPLE I BEG TO INFORM YOU THAT IN COURSE OF CONVERSATIONS BETWEEN VIETNAM GOVERNMENT AND FRENCH REPRESENTATIVES THE LATTER REQUIRE THE SECESSION OF COCHINCHINA AND THE RETURN OF FRENCH TROOPS IN HANOI STOP MEANWHILE FRENCH POPULATION AND TROOPS ARE MAKING ACTIVE PREPARATIONS FOR A COUP DE MAIN IN HANOI AND FOR MILLTARY AGGRESSION STOP I THEREFORE MOST EARNESTLY APPEAL TO YOU PERSONALLY AND TO THE AMERICAN PEOPLE TO INTERFERE URGENTLY IN SUPPORT OF OUR INDEPENDENCE AND HELP MAKING THE NEGOTIATIONS MORE IN KEEPING WITH THE PRINCIPLES OF THE ATLANTIC AND SAN FRANCISCO CHARTERS

RESPECTFULLY

HOCHIMINH

Hochiminh

Ho Chi Minh's telegram to US President Truman in 1946 appealing for aid in Vietnam's struggle for independence from the French.

town of Dien Bien Phu, close to the border between northern Vietnam and Laos, entirely dependent on airborne supplies, in the belief that French tanks and mobile troops, on terrain of their own choosing, could threaten the Vietminh. Navarre's choosing was disastrously bad, even ignoring the rains and swampy ground and a cloud-covered airstrip. And General Giap amazingly turned the tables on Navarre by amassing much larger forces than ever expected there to besiege the garrison by secretly manhandling artillery, ammunition and supplies through hidden mountain trails until the Vietminh forces had vastly superior strength, a three-to-one advantage in manpower, when they moved from siege of Dien Bien Phu to an all-out attack in early March. The French were shocked to find their garrison and crucial airstrip coming under heavy artillery fire from the surrounding hillsides. It soon became clear that Dien Bien Phu was doomed. The French artillery commander committed suicide out of sheer mortification.

Ho Chi Minh (with General Vo Nguyen Giap, commander of the Vietminh forces) planning the battle of Dien Bien Phu.

The French appealed to the US government for both financial and military assistance in April, and for some weeks, the prospect of American air and ground force intervention there was under serious consideration in Washington, including airstrikes with 'tactical' nuclear weapons from two US aircraft carriers which were moved into nearby waters. Fortunately, saner counsels prevailed. But the secretary of state, John Foster Dulles, was already thinking about wider 'joint action' against the Vietminh (along similar lines to that which had been invoked by a unique UN resolution over the Korean War in mid-1950) in ominous terms. All that caused Nehru, in particular, deep concern as to their implications for global conflict and the external pressure that

THE GENEVA CONFERENCE AND VIETNAM

Because the Geneva Conference coincided with both the historic battle of Dien Bien Phu and the Colombo Conference, which is of such importance in our story of how the Bandung meeting came about, its significance in the international politics of 1954–5 needs to be explained. The battle of Dien Bien Phu achieved an end to the first Vietnam War—between the French and the Vietminh—after nine years of conflict. Yet, the terms of the Geneva Accords also paved the way for the second phase of the war, involving the Americans increasingly and directly after 1964. The Geneva Conference lasted nearly 10 weeks and had moments of high drama as well as dour, tedious bargaining by such senior statesmen as Sir Anthony Eden, Vyacheslav Molotov, Zhou Enlai, Georges Bidault and Pham Van Dong (though not Dulles, who refused to attend more than the opening ceremony, or to shake hands with Zhou). And it focused world attention on Asian issues in an unprecedented way.

All the participants except the Americans were eager to help find a formula for a peaceful settlement of the Vietnam conflict which would be acceptable in both Hanoi and Paris. (The US did not want to see a settlement that would be tantamount to a Vietminh takeover of the whole country, either immediately or later.) Pham Van Dong believed that, on the strength of the great victory the Vietminh had just won at Dien Bien Phu, it was entitled to a political settlement favourable to Hanoi that reflected it. He demanded a political settlement before a ceasefire, a French withdrawal from her colonies there, and recognition of the communist *Pathet Lao* and Free Khmer resistance movements (rather than what he regarded as French 'puppet' governments there). Zhou was less concerned with backing those demands than with ensuring that there would be no opportunity for the Americans to intervene in Vietnam or to take the place of the French as they were pushed out of Indochina. 'We are here to re-establish peace, not to back the Vietminh', he told a French delegate in private. Molotov too wanted to help the French get off the hook in Vietnam, for reasons to do with European politics, so he was looking towards a compromise, as was Eden. The deadlock persisted until the French Parliament voted out the Laniel government in mid-June and chose as prime

would be put on countries like India.

Dien Bien Phu was overrun by Giap's forces on 7 May when the French garrison had no choice but to surrender. Its fall marked the final collapse of French colonial rule in Indochina. It also ushered in a phase of intense political uncertainty for the three 'Associated States'—South Vietnam (soon to be called the 'State of Vietnam'), Cambodia and Laos—as French dominance gave way gradually to American.

The Geneva and Colombo Conferences

At almost the same time, a major international conference of the big powers involved in the Korean War, including China, had begun at Geneva on 26 April 1954 with the aim of negotiating a political settlement to supplement the ceasefire in Korea. It had been planned some months earlier and the French later asked that consideration of the

minister Pierre Mendès-France, a long-time opponent of the war. He accepted office with a promise that, if he could not negotiate a satisfactory solution at Geneva within four weeks, he would resign. That put pressure on Pham to negotiate a compromise formula, which Zhou and Molotov also wanted badly. Pham found himself obliged to drop his demand for a peace settlement first, to accept a partition of Vietnam, and finally to give way also on the partition line, which was drawn at the 17th parallel, much further north than Pham had wished. The partition was intended to be merely temporary, pending elections to unify the former colony, but after the new US-backed Southern leader, Ngo Dinh Diem, refused to accept the Geneva Accords, it turned out to be semi-permanent until 1975.

The Geneva Accords were more favourable to the French than they had dared hope initially. There was to be a ceasefire and withdrawal of French troops from north of the partition line and of Vietminh troops from the south, but not the political settlement Pham had been demanding. Elections were to be held only after a two-year interval (Pham had at first agreed only to a six-month wait), which deprived the Vietminh of the opportunity to cash in on the momentum of their military victory. The French and the DRV (Democratic Republic of Vietnam) signed the agreement, with the other participants merely giving oral endorsement. The US merely agreed to abide by it.

As the French pulled out over the next two years and the US became more deeply involved there through its support for the Diem regime in the south (the 'State of Vietnam'), much argument arose about the intent of the Geneva Accords. But they had achieved the important goals of ending the first anti-colonial war in Vietnam and marking a big step towards full independence for Cambodia and Laos, as well as the divided Vietnam.

Vietnam crisis be added to it. The discussions on Korea quickly ran into a deadlock and were suspended, but the negotiations on Vietnam lasted from early May until mid-July. After a lot of intense bargaining, they finally resulted in the Geneva Accords, embodying the partition of Vietnam, meant only to be a temporary arrangement, as specified there. The details of those negotiations are of little relevance to our story here, except in two respects.

One was the central role played by Zhou Enlai as a mediator between the French and the Vietminh. The other was the pressure he applied to Pham Van Dong, the Vietminh delegate, to come to terms with the French and to moderate his demands—pressure which later led Pham to complain, 'He double-crossed me'. Zhou's primary aim at Geneva was to bring about a peace settlement, not to help Pham Van Dong maximise the political benefits flowing from the Vietminh's military victory. Above all, he wanted to avoid a situation which might give rise to US military intervention in the French colonial war, for that would simply have replicated the dangers China had experienced in Korea, with US troops massed at her frontiers and contemplating air or military strikes upon China herself. Zhou succeeded on the military side of that aim, although the Americans were in due course to insinuate themselves politically into the position of dominance vacated by the French in South Vietnam and ensure a continuation of both political and later military conflict there for the next 20 years.

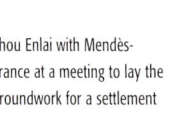

Zhou Enlai with Mendès-France at a meeting to lay the groundwork for a settlement of the Vietnam crisis.

Almost simultaneous with the Geneva Conference, a much smaller meeting of leaders of five newly independent Asian nations—India, Ceylon, Pakistan, Burma and Indonesia— took place in Colombo. This meeting had little direct bearing on the course of events at Geneva or on the political settlement ultimately achieved there, but the problems involved in reaching the Geneva settlement, which seemed immensely forbidding at the time of the Colombo meeting, became the meeting's main focus of attention. But the Colombo Conference had greater significance as the almost unwitting starting-point for the various negotiations which were to lead in due course to the Bandung conference nearly 12 months later, as we shall see. For it was at Colombo that Ali Sastroamidjojo, the Indonesian prime minister, first floated to the others of the 'Colombo Five' his proposal for a wider gathering of leaders of Asian and African nations to coordinate their strategies in the dangerous Cold War atmosphere that had developed. It was also an opportunity for 'the voice of Asia to be heard', which Sir John Kotelawala had called for earlier in the year as the Vietnam crisis was boiling up. As such, it was a small-scale precursor to Bandung.

SEATO AND CENTO

The origins of the Southeast Asian Treaty Organisation, SEATO, can be traced back to a call by Dulles on 29 March 1954 for 'united action' to resist the expansion of communism in Vietnam, just as the intensification of the Vietminh assault on Dien Bien Phu was casting grave doubts on the survival of the French garrison there. Despite his efforts over the next few weeks to draw the British and other allies into military support for the French there, the British government firmly resisted his pressure to engage them—partly because Sir Anthony Eden wanted to see what progress towards a negotiated settlement in Vietnam could be made at the upcoming Geneva Conference. But as a sop to Dulles, Eden floated the idea of a Southeast Asian collective security agreement involving the US, Britain, her Commonwealth partners and other Asian countries. Intensive negotiations took place over the next four months, during and after the Geneva Conference, but only the 'white' dominions—Australia and New Zealand—and three Asian nations closely associated with the US—Pakistan, the Philippines and Thailand—responded favourably. India, Indonesia, Burma and Ceylon all firmly declined. A meeting of the participating nations was held in Manila in September to negotiate the Manila Agreement, of which SEATO was the military component. Early expectations that SEATO would be analogous to NATO were derailed when the operative clause regarding action to be taken in the event of aggression towards another member was qualified by the phrase 'will act in accordance with its constitutional processes' (i.e. in the US case, after consultations with the Congress) rather than by automatic action as in the NATO treaty. Dulles' hopes of engaging South Vietnam, Cambodia and Laos in SEATO had to be abandoned because of the terms of the Geneva Accords, although a vague umbrella clause referring to action under SEATO in defence of them was inserted. SEATO was often cited later as a justification for US involvement in the Vietnam conflict, although it was never formally invoked.

CENTO, the Central Treaty Organisation, was the name later applied to the 1955 Baghdad Pact, a military cooperation agreement between Turkey, Iraq, Iran, Pakistan and Britain. It was an extension of a Pact of Mutual Cooperation negotiated between Turkey and Iraq in February 1954. The US also became a participant later, and it was hoped that other Arab League nations might also be induced to join, but that did not happen. It formed part of a US-led network of anti-communist collective security treaties to contain the Soviet Union and China at that time. But Dulles was less strongly committed to CENTO than to SEATO because of the complex politics and rivalries among the Middle Eastern nations. His enthusiasm for it waned not long afterwards.

Romulo (far right) with President Osmeña (centre) and the Americans (left to right), Rear Admiral Daniel Barbey, Major General Walter Kreuger, and Admiral Thomas Kincaid, just before the landing in Leyte.

ZHOU ENLAI (1898–1976)

Zhou was not only the star of the Bandung conference but also its chief beneficiary. He succeeded brilliantly in changing the image of the previously isolated PRC in the eyes of other Asian and African leaders, making it possible for China to develop new diplomatic initiatives later in the 1950s, which contributed to lessening her dependence on the Soviet Union. Zhou had more experience in foreign affairs than any other member of the Chinese leadership and was a very shrewd operator in domestic politics as well.

Nehru wrote that at Bandung, Zhou displayed 'ability and moderation… Whenever he spoke he did so with authority'. He was obviously anxious that the conference should succeed and tried to be as accommodating as possible. 'He was patient even when he had to put up with offensive behaviour.'

He was not yet well known outside China until the Geneva and Bandung conferences, but he achieved wide recognition there as a skilful diplomat and pragmatic negotiator, although also a strongly committed communist. He had earlier played an active part in political negotiations with opponents during the civil war in China, when he was one of the most senior first-generation members of the Chinese Communist Party (CPC). Stanley Karnow wrote that he

> showed at Geneva for the first time the skills that made him one of the most brilliant diplomats of the century. Urbane, subtle, tough and determined, he was a unique blend of Chinese mandarin and Communist commissar, and he had a special affinity for France, having spent his youth in Paris…

Born to a wealthy scholar-class family and educated in Japan and Paris, Zhou joined the CPC in 1922, and during the phase of cooperation with the KMT was Political Director at the Whampoa Military Academy in Guangdong. He was then a rival to Mao for the party leadership and their relations were badly strained in the early 1930s when the Party came under heavy police pressure following a break with the KMT. But during the terrible Long March to Yen-an in 1934–5, Mao gained control of the party apparatus and thereafter Zhou served him faithfully to the end of his life.

After the establishment of the PRC in October 1949, Zhou became premier and foreign minister, negotiating the Sino-Soviet Treaty of Friendship with Stalin in 1950 and later the Geneva Accords with the French and others at the Geneva Conference in 1954.

One of his most important achievements at Bandung was the Zhou Enlai–Sunario Agreement on the Dual Nationality issue of the overseas Chinese in Indonesia, under which China abandoned its earlier insistence that they were Chinese nationals by virtue of their descent. Although it took some time (and many troubles) before the issue was fully resolved with Indonesia and the other Southeast Asian countries, that concession was a major step along the way towards an eventual settlement of the legal and political problems at stake.

Zhou remained the foremost of Mao's lieutenants during the 20 years after Bandung, although he stepped down as foreign minister in 1958 and played only intermittent diplomatic roles thereafter. He was generally regarded as a leader of the 'moderate' faction in the CPC during the internal turmoils of the (disastrous) Great Leap Forward and the Cultural Revolution, but because he clung so tenaciously to 'the Great Helmsman', who often sided with the radicals, he was regarded with some suspicion by both sides in his later years. When he died, however, there was a great popular outpouring of grief. His achievements as foreign minister were beyond question.

US-China antagonism in 1954–1955

The Cold War was at a particularly dangerous stage in 1954–5 for various reasons, any one of which might have triggered a hot war, potentially nuclear, between the two rival powers. The Vietnam crisis was the most immediate and precarious source of such conflict, which the Geneva Conference managed to defuse by a hair's breadth. But other risks persisted even after that. The Taiwan Straits issue arose first when the US deployed its Seventh Fleet there at the start of the Korean War in 1950 to protect Chiang Kai-shek's KMT forces which had fled to Taiwan; it came to the fore again soon after the Korean and Vietnam Wars began to wane. Nuclear testing and the escalation of the nuclear arms race were also ever-present worries, for Russia had exploded its first hydrogen bomb in 1953. But most relevant to any consideration of peace or war in Asia was the tense state of US-China relations throughout the 1950s and Washington's determination to isolate the communist regime in Beijing and demonise it in the eyes of the world.

The refusal of the US to recognise Mao's government in October 1949 (and its anger towards those of its allies that did) became even more stubborn as time passed instead of less, as was earlier hoped. For China was not only being denied what she regarded as her rightful place in the UN and on the Security Council, still occupied by the KMT rump regime in Taiwan until the 1970s, but was subjected to a policy of 'containment' by the creation of collective security alliances around her similar to those the US was also creating to the west and south of the Soviet Union. More seriously, the presence of the US Seventh Fleet in the Taiwan Straits to prevent any Chinese attempt to attack Taiwan ('liberate' was Beijing's word for it) created an acutely precarious and perilous situation. Threats of US retaliation if China tried to attack caused both the Beijing and Taipei regimes to resort to dangerous brinkmanship in their threats against each other.

A US propaganda poster targeted at Chinese soldiers during the Korean War; the admonition in Chinese reads, 'Death is near'.

JOHN FOSTER DULLES: 'NEUTRALISM IS IMMORAL'

The spectre of John Foster Dulles hovered over the various international crises of 1954–5 (and even over the Bandung conference itself) like Banquo's ghost, implacable and inescapable. Because of his starkly bipolar view of the world order, which he saw as divided between one side that was essentially evil and the other unquestionably good, he refused to contemplate any compromise between them, and he put immense pressure on the uncommitted governments of Asia to go along with his thinking and join SEATO or CENTO. Compromise between the two camps, or the thought that some alternative approach might be possible–a 'third way', such as Nehru was advocating–was simply anathema to him. Few dared to reject him; although even those delegates at Bandung who were bound by Western security pacts showed little or no adherence to his sharply polarised worldview.

Whether or not he actually used the phrase 'neutralism is immoral' in so many words is unclear, but he undoubtedly said that 'the principal of neutrality…has become an obsolete conception…an immoral…and short-sighted concept'. Hoopes shows in an illuminating book, The

Devil and John Foster Dulles, that the frame of mind behind this kind of thinking–and the uncompromisingly rigid set of policies adopted by the US on Cold War issues under his leadership between 1953 and 1958, even to the trivial extent of refusing to send greetings to the AA Conference (as the Soviet leaders sensibly did)–were all of a piece with the rigidity of his morality. To him, communism was so evil that any compromise with it was indefensible.

The self-righteous moralism that underlay his thinking made it impossible for him to consider any possibility of compromise with communist 'evildoers'. He had experienced a religious conversion in the 1930s (after several highly lucrative decades as a corporate lawyer, and a personal crisis about the drift of world affairs), which reinforced what Finer (by no means a radical) called his 'monumental self-righteousness [as] a newborn Calvinist who was a deeply committed pillar of the Christian church'. Although a highly intelligent man and well-informed foreign policy thinker, he could also be amazingly petty and truculent, as in the case of his abrupt withdrawal of an earlier offer to help fund Egypt's

The tensions that developed over the Taiwan Straits issue were a matter of great concern worldwide over a period of roughly eight months before the Bandung conference, for any miscalculation by either side could have led to war. The situation was aggravated by the position of the two offshore islands, Quemoy and Matsu, which were still occupied by KMT troops and very close to the Chinese mainland near Amoy (now called Xiamen)—so close that they were not defended by the shield provided by the Seventh Fleet, hence highly vulnerable to Chinese attack if it came. Fortunately, Zhou defused the crisis at Bandung with a public offer to talk peace with Washington if it would respond. But Washington did not.

At a deeper level, the puzzle about US-China relations during the years before Bandung leads back to a question about why the antagonism on both sides was so intractable. Washington seemed

construction of the High Dam at Aswan in July 1956, which precipitated Nasser's decision to nationalise the Suez Canal to pay for it. That in turn gave rise to the war between Egypt and Britain, France and Israel (not backed by Dulles) a few months later. Dulles suspected that Nasser was blackmailing the US by hinting that Soviet aid would be available if American finance was refused, so he said without a moment's reflection, 'Well, if you have the money already you don't need any from us. My offer is withdrawn.' He was outraged by the very notion of the US being blackmailed. Moreover, the opportunity to thwart and humiliate Nasser delighted him, without any regard for the consequences.

Ironically, he was very critical also of the colonial powers, the French in particular, just as Roosevelt had been, because he thought they were helping the cause of communism by resisting their colonies' progress towards independence. But in his refusal to see any good in neutralism or non-alignment, he put himself in a position of such opposition to what Bandung was all about that he simply overlooked the important shift in the tides of world politics in the later 1950s that it had generated.

Richard Goold-Adams has posed the questions: Was he great or disastrous as secretary of state in those critical years? Did his famous brinkmanship take the world to the edge of an abyss, or save it from going over? The verdict he offers is equivocal. Dulles may have been right in his hardline approach to the Russians at that point of the nuclear stand-off. But because his personality made it impossible for him to balance an ingrained anti-colonialism—coupled with a distrust of the European powers whose colonial policies he saw as playing into the hands of the Russians—with his views on the 'immorality of neutralism' and compromise, generally, he managed to make the worst of both worlds. 'His puritanical view of both colonialism and neutralism, and the even greater sin of Communism... could not make him condone lesser evils.' But at Bandung, it was the idea of an alternative way between the two polarised Cold War camps that won the day.

utterly unwilling to compromise or offer any concessions for the sake of achieving a détente. To some extent that derived from the personality and utterly rigid mindset of the secretary of state, John Foster Dulles, who seemed to regard compromise or taking up a non-aligned stance as implying the acceptance of evil. But it was also due to the political atmosphere of the McCarthyist witch-hunt across the US in the early 1950s, when anyone who could be blamed for the 'loss of China' to communism was hounded mercilessly. No one wanted to be blamed similarly for the 'loss of Vietnam' or the rest of Southeast Asia if the domino theory proved correct. The Bandung conference occurred against the backdrop of that attitude in the US, and one of its greater successes was that it succeeded in convincing people in many countries that there was indeed a 'third way' and that the Dulles approach was outdated.

TIMELINE: 1945–1955

1945
- Atomic bomb attacks on Hiroshima and Nagasaki in August: Japan surrenders.
- Indonesia proclaims independence: the military and diplomatic struggle to achieve it lasts till her sovereignty is officially recognised in December 1949.
- Vietminh struggle against the French (the 'French Indochina War') begins; it lasts till 1955.
- Korea is divided in August–September into US and Russian segments.

Churchill, Roosevelt and Stalin at the Yalta Conference in 1945, the last cordial meeting of the wartime Big Three before the Cold War set in.

1946
- The Philippines granted independence by the US on 4 July.

1947
- India and Pakistan obtain independence from Britain in August: the partition leads to intense communal violence.

1948
- Cold War intensifies as the 'Iron Curtain' hardens, resulting in the Berlin Airlift, and Soviet intervention in Hungary and Czechoslovakia.
- Communist insurgencies in Southeast Asia against newly independent 'bourgeois nationalist' regimes and liberation movements, notably in Burma, Malaya ('The Emergency', till 1960), the Philippines (Hukbalahap rebellion, lasting to the mid-1950s), and Indonesia (the Madiun revolt).
- Ceylon and Burma gain independence.

1949
- Arms race intensifies: Soviet Union gets atomic bomb; US develops hydrogen bomb, nuclear arms tests conducted on Bikini Atoll and Eniwetok in the Marshall Islands.
- NATO is established in July to prevent Soviet attack on Europe.
- People's Republic of China (PRC) is established in October under Mao Zedong after the Chinese communists win the civil war.
- Transfer of sovereignty to Indonesia by the Dutch in December; general recognition of her independence.
- Military and political stalemate occurs in Vietnam as the French concede partial self-rule to Vietnam, Cambodia and Laos; the Vietminh is excluded.

1950
- Korean War: UN-US action to prevent communist North Korea from overrunning South Korea; Chinese troops support the North, nearly overrunning the UN forces in the South.

A South Korean infantry officer on patrol during the Korean War.

1951
- Korean War threatens to spread to China; military stalemate develops.

1952
- Egypt and Sudan are promised independence.
- Libya gains independence from Italy in February.
- Japan Peace Treaty signed in April: US security treaties with Japan, Australia-New Zealand (ANZUS) and the Philippines.
- Korean War still deadlocked; in the US, Eisenhower elected on a pledge to achieve an end to war by negotiation or escalation.
- Egypt's King Farouk is overthrown by military junta in July; Nasser emerges gradually as the strong man.

1952
- French colonies in North Africa—Tunisia, Morocco and Algeria—press for independence.
- Mau-Mau insurgency in Kenya is suppressed by force: blacks in South Africa struggle against apartheid
- Neocolonialism and white racialism are under fire everywhere.

1953
- Korean armistice enacted at Panmunjon in July.
- In Paris, the Laniel government starts to consider an end to war in Vietnam through negotiations from strength; the Navarre Plan is devised as a means to inflict decisive defeat on the Vietminh, but it backfires at Dien Bien Phu.

1954
- Dien Bien Phu comes under siege by General Giap's forces; a major attack is launched on 13 March; the French request for US intervention is refused by Eisenhower, resulting in a major French defeat on 7 May when Dien Bien Phu falls, signalling the end of the French colonial empire in Asia.
- Geneva Conference on Korean peace settlement and Vietnam War opens on 26 April.
- Colombo Conference on 28 April; first public consideration there of Indonesia's proposal for an Asian-African Conference of newly independent nations.
- Negotiations at Geneva last from May through July; Laniel government replaced by Mendès-France administration, with commitment to end the Vietnam War in four weeks.
- Geneva Accords signed 20 July, resulting in a de facto partition of Vietnam
- Zhou Enlai visits Nehru in New Delhi: they agree on the *Panch Shila* principles of peaceful coexistence.
- Manila Conference in September: SEATO created.
- Ali Sastroamidjojo meets Nehru in New Delhi; they reach an agreement to hold the AA Conference soon, suggest holding another meeting of the Colombo Five in Indonesia to make arrangements for it.
- Bogor Conference from 28 to 30 December.

Dulles in his limousine during the Geneva Conference.

1955
- Invitations to attend the Bandung AA Conference are issued in January; acceptances gradually follow.
- Taiwan Straits crisis between PRC and US intensifies between January and April to a dangerous level.
- Asia-Africa Conference at Bandung meets 18–25 April.

American forces land in Inchon harbour during the Korean War.

MAKING IT HAPPEN:
FROM COLOMBO TO BOGOR TO BANDUNG

While Ali Sastroamidjojo deserves the credit for first putting forward the idea of a meeting of African and Asian leaders, it was the Colombo Conference which gave him the opportunity to do so. That conference was the brainchild of Ceylon's Sir John Kotelawala, who initially had no such outcome in mind. He had earlier felt simply that

> it was time the united voice of Asia was heard in the councils of the world whose destinies had hitherto tended to be controlled almost entirely from another direction.

International developments made the meeting more important than Sir John had earlier imagined, and 'Colombo was followed by Bogor, and Bogor by Bandung. What a chain reaction, and what a climax'.

The Colombo Conference, as suggested by Sir John, was intended to be a very informal affair, without any specific agenda in advance, and essentially just a 'neighbours' group' to enable the leaders to get to know each other better. But by the time they met, the Vietnam situation overshadowed everything else. Inevitably, the 'Colombo Five' (the term used here in preference to the more usual 'Colombo Powers') were greatly concerned with the danger of a wider war developing there. The topics discussed, according to Sir John, were 'broad and universal in character: the situation in Indochina, the hydrogen bomb, colonialism and racialism, international communism, and economic cooperation in Southeast Asia'.

In his speech at the opening of the Colombo meeting, Ali Sastroamidjojo asked: 'Where do we nations of Asia stand now? Do we want to be dragged into this power dispute? We are truly at a crossroads in the history of mankind.' As a provisional answer, he suggested 'another and more comprehensive conference, because the problems of colonialism were worldwide and involved also the peoples of Asia and of Africa'.

A stream and bridge on the grounds of the Istana Bogor, a tranquil setting for the Bogor Conference.

But Nehru was primarily concerned at that time with the precarious situation in Vietnam, on which he proposed they move with great caution since it could not be solved immediately, the most pressing problem to be resolved at Geneva being a ceasefire. Nehru urged that France hand over full sovereignty there, but the question of who should receive it was a complex one, best left to the Geneva consultations about to take place.

Ali later wrote that 'the chance to put my proposal came only in the sixth session… [O]n the whole it was well received, although not enthusiastically'. (He does not mention whether at that stage he had suggested a meeting of only the leaders of Asian and African countries represented in the UN, as Kahin indicates, which would not have included China, or a more broadly inclusive gathering.) Nehru took the view that while there were good points in his proposal, many problems would have to be overcome if such a conference was to achieve the consensus that was essential in order to make an impact, since there were such great differences of opinion among the likely participants. He hoped 'it would not get stuck halfway'. Was China to be invited? And who else? Much high-level preparation would clearly be needed. Yet Nehru's support for the idea was crucial because of his international prestige at that time.

The Colombo Five prime ministers—(from left to right) Burma's U Nu, India's Jawaharlal Nehru, Ceylon's Sir John Kotelawala, Indonesia's Ali Sastroamidjojo, and Pakistan's Mohammed Ali—at the conference in Colombo in April 1954.

It was interesting to observe the personalities of my distinguished colleagues—Nehru, earnest disinterested, fiery; Mohammed Ali, debonair, forceful, practical; Nu, serene, dispassionate, brief, but very much to the point; Ali Sastroamidjojo, courteous, understanding, dedicated.

– Sir John Kotelawala on the other Colombo Five prime ministers

But all the conference communiqué had to say on the subject, in its final clause, was:

> The prime ministers discussed the possibility of holding a conference of African-Asian nations and favoured a proposal that the Prime Minister of Indonesia might explore the possibility of such a conference.

That was an 'obvious diplomatic understatement', Ali Sastroamidjojo later wrote, 'showing the four prime ministers' doubts about [its] feasibility'. Their responses had been lukewarm at best. The political problems involved seemed altogether too formidable to be worth trying to tackle at such a time. Within eight months, however, the idea had begun to take shape sufficiently to warrant a further meeting of the Colombo Five at Bogor in December to determine how best to proceed with such a

SIR JOHN LIONEL KOTELAWALA, C.H., K.B.E., LL.D. (1897–1980)

Apart from being the man who had convened the Colombo Conference at which the seed of the idea of an Afro-Asian gathering was planted by Ali Sastroamidjojo, and thereafter being one of the five sponsors of the Bandung meeting, Sir John's role at Bandung was noteworthy mainly for the uproar he caused when he overtly condemned Soviet 'colonialism' in Eastern Europe and provoked Zhou Enlai into an agitated response which greatly alarmed the Indonesian organisers. (He later made peace with Zhou without much fuss.) But he was not one of the more hardline anti-communists or pro-US delegates at Bandung, being closer in outlook to Sir Anthony Eden than John Foster Dulles; and while Ceylon was not a member of the non-aligned camp in his day, it never joined SEATO either.

He comes across in his mildly engaging autobiography, *An Asian Prime Minister Speaks*, as a somewhat self-promoting member of Ceylon's Anglophile elite, who rose to prominence as a civil servant under British rule after concluding his education at Cambridge, and who later became an elected member of Parliament and president of the (rather conservative) United National Party after independence. He seemed to rejoice in his knighthood, membership of the Privy Council and other high honours in a way that the other Colombo Five leaders would have found laughably inappropriate in a good nationalist. Ali Sastroamidjojo, who seemed to like him personally, later inscribed a book for him 'to the most undiplomatic diplomat I have ever known'.

JAWAHARLAL NEHRU (1889–1964)

As prime minister of India from the time it achieved independence in August 1947 until his death in 1964, Pandit Nehru (as he was commonly called, the word *pandit* meaning 'a learned man') was regarded almost universally as the foremost of all the leaders of the newly independent nations of Asia. His record as a long-time opponent of British colonial rule in India, one who had spent nearly nine years in prison and was the closest associate of the revered Mahatma Gandhi ('India's most illustrious son since the Buddha', says Brecher–*Mahatma* meaning 'Great Soul') gave him a special standing in the company of the other Asian nationalists.

Born into an aristocratic Kashmiri family, Nehru was educated at Harrow, Cambridge and the Inns of Court in London before he returned to India and was plunged into the struggle for independence under Gandhi's leadership, embracing the masses and enduring prison gladly. He was a unique blend of Eastern and Western values and ideas. Austere and rather puritanical, meditating or doing yoga every day yet also reading widely, he developed a fascinating but almost unfathomable personality, very different from those of other prominent Asian nationalists. Politically a moderate, mildly socialist in an undoctrinaire way, a convinced democrat and a strong advocate of a secular state, he put his stamp on the new Indian polity in an indelible way.

As head of the world's largest democratic country, he had steered India out of the horrific communal violence of 1947–8 that resulted from the partition of the former British colony into India and Pakistan. He then led her through her first ever nationwide elections under universal suffrage in 1952–a feat many sceptics had doubted was possible with a population of nearly 350 million. By the time of the Bandung conference, he had led his country to become a modern, democratic, secular state, a beacon to the rest of Asia. He was highly articulate, a skilled and experienced organiser, a far-sighted statesman as well as a shrewd politician, and above all a spellbinding orator. He had a wide appeal to the Indian masses as well as to the brightest and best of people around the world.

At Bandung, he and Zhou Enlai stood out as most influential of the key figures who contributed to its successful outcome–Nehru the intellectual architect of non-alignment, Zhou the deft conciliator between divergent groups of nations. 'Nehru was in the background, quiet, studied', wrote Richard Wright. He made only one or two major speeches, but several crucial interjections. His plan to use the conference to bring China into the Asian community of newly independent nations worked well, although his hopes of recruiting many more nations to sign on to the five principles of the *Panch Shila* and non-alignment were less successful. (The *Dasa Sila Bandung*, the Ten Bandung Principles, never achieved the international public attention that the *Panch Shila* had in 1954, and even the latter also lost their gloss soon after that.) But Nehru was certainly the uncrowned king of the non-aligned nations until the early 1960s. His direct political influence among them waned after the 1961 Belgrade Conference, as Egypt's Nasser and Tito of Yugoslavia came to the fore within it, with a different set of aims for the movement, which were much more anti-imperialist and potentially radical.

The tragedy of his life was the Sino-Indian border war of 1962, which shattered his hopes of friendship between the two countries and the goal of Asian-African unity. He died less than 18 months later.

ALI SASTROAMIDJOJO (1903–1976)

Ali Sastroamidjojo, prime minister of Indonesia in 1953–5 and 1956–7, had conceived of the idea of a conference of leaders of the newly independent Asian and African nations while he was Indonesia's ambassador at the UN and in Washington in 1950–53. When he was designated prime minister in August 1953, he gave closer attention to it as the key element in his government's new aim of a more 'active and independent' foreign policy.

Ali was one of that generation of Indonesian students in the Netherlands in the 1920s who established the first nationalist organisation there, the PPI (*Perhimpoenan Peladjar Indonesia*, the Indonesian Students' Association), and he had contact with the League Against Imperialism. He was closely associated with some of the Indonesians who attended the Bierville and Brussels congresses in 1926–7. He became active in nationalist organisations after he returned to Java in 1928, and in 1945, was among the leadership group of the PNI (*Partai Nasional Indonesia*), the party most closely associated with Sukarno, the foremost nationalist leader.

He was not personally or politically very close to Sukarno, being of a more

cautious, even conservative disposition. He had been a minister of education in one of the first post-independence cabinets and a member of the Indonesian delegation to the Round Table Conference in The Hague to negotiate the transfer of sovereignty in 1949, so he was a senior and experienced politician. His high standing in the PNI can be seen in the fact that when the PNI was called upon to form a government in 1953, he was called back urgently from Washington to do so. In 1956–7, he was again prime minister in the coalition government formed after Indonesia's first national elections in 1955. When that government fell in April 1957 as a consequence of regional revolts, and President Sukarno moved to 'bury the political parties' (and parliamentary democracy), Ali again became Indonesia's ambassador to the UN from 1957 to 1960.

He remained an influential member of the PNI for many years after that, at the head of its less radical wing, but was never again as prominent in political life. His role as the initiator of the Afro-Asian Conference and the Conference Chairman was the high point in his long career as a leading Indonesian nationalist.

meeting and work out its basic rationale, objectives, procedures and membership. The reasons why that change of heart occurred constitute an important part of the background to the Bandung story.

The Parliament House in Colombo, venue of the Colombo Conference.

From Colombo to Bogor

The progress made over that time, from initial scepticism to strong endorsement, was due in part to shifts in the international situation that were occurring then, and in part to the persistence of Ali Sastroamidjojo himself. (He had strong reasons of domestic politics to want to bring his idea to fruition, having put great stress on more positive action to give effect to Indonesia's 'free and active' foreign policy of non-alignment or neutrality on Cold War issues when he first became prime minister in August 1953.) Fortunately for him, developments in the wider world between May and September were to have a major influence in making the idea of an AA gathering more feasible, particularly by shifting Nehru's thoughts on the matter with reference to the part it might play in bringing about China's acceptance into the world community.

> ### PANCH SHILA
>
> The Five Principles of peaceful coexistence, as established by Nehru and Zhou Enlai, were:
> - *Mutual respect for each other's territorial integrity and sovereignty*
> - *Mutual non-aggression*
> - *Mutual non-interference in each other's internal affairs*
> - *Equality and mutual benefit*
> - *Peaceful coexistence*
>
> They were first stated in the preamble to the Sino-Indian Agreement on Tibet of 30 April 1954 (a time of remarkable events worldwide), with no elaboration beyond the above definition.

The Colombo Five at Bogor.

Two developments were crucial. Zhou Enlai stopped at New Delhi in mid-year for talks with Nehru and the two established a cordial personal and political relationship which gave rise to their adoption of the Five Principles of coexistence, *Panch Shila*, as the basis for future bilateral relations between them. Why the China-India relationship began to blossom at this time (it became the heyday of the phrase '*Hindi-Chini Bhai-Bhai*', or 'India and China are brothers') need not concern us here, but it was singularly fortunate for Ali Sastroamidjojo's purposes, although it did not immediately swing Nehru round to his view on an AA conference. The other development that was pushing in that direction was the pressure being applied by the US and Britain upon the newly independent nations of Asia to join what was at first called the Collective Defence Agreement in Southeast Asia, later known as SEATO. India and Indonesia were both urged to join and both declined. But this political state of affairs led Ali to write to Nehru in mid-August about the 'tense world situation' and the relevance of his proposal to it. Nehru's reply still indicated a 'cautious and lukewarm attitude' but he invited Ali to Delhi to discuss it further.

Before they met in late September, the Manila Agreement establishing SEATO had been signed, with only three Asian participants—Pakistan, the Philippines and Thailand—and at US insistence, clauses extending its coverage to Vietnam, Cambodia and Laos in certain circumstances, despite the fact that the governments of

BOGOR

The choice of Bogor, about 50 km south of Jakarta and 80 km northwest of Bandung, for the meeting of the Colombo Five to make their final arrangements for the Bandung conference was due mainly to the fact that the Istana Bogor, the presidential palace there, was a suitably imposing and convenient venue for such a meeting of five heads of state as guests of the president of Indonesia. It was the only such high-level meeting ever held there so far. Appropriately, the smooth progress of the December 1954 meeting reflected the tranquil atmosphere of the place.

Formerly the hill country residence of the Dutch Governor-General, the Istana is a large and gracious old building, located at the edge of the famous Bogor botanical gardens, one of the most beautiful scenic spots in Java. President Sukarno made frequent use of it. Curiously, his successor, President Suharto, rarely did, shunning it entirely after an exceptionally violent storm in 1970 caused severe damage to trees in the gardens, which one of his spiritual advisors warned him would be a bad omen for him.

The Istana Bogor with its large lily pond (below); the majestic gates of the Bogor botanical gardens (left).

*Much will depend on whether Peking considers itself as more
Asian than communist, or vice versa...*
– Times of India, 28 December 1954

those countries were precluded by the Geneva Accords from joining.
(Krishna Menon, India's first High Commissioner to Britain, referred to
it as a reversion to the 'spheres of influence' policies of the colonial
powers in earlier times.) When Ali arrived in New Delhi, he found
Nehru initially as lukewarm as before towards his proposal, but Nehru
changed his mind after Ali had addressed the Indian Council of World
Affairs and the Indian Parliament on the subject, getting warm
encouragement from both bodies. Ali stressed its advantages as a means

U NU (1907–1995)

U Nu, prime minister of Burma, was a quiet, unassuming man, devoutly Buddhist, and one of the most likeable delegates to the Bandung conference in the eyes of many. He was widely respected there and beyond for his ideology and principles, which had much in common with Nehru's, while his demeanour was far less dominating. As one of the sponsoring prime ministers of the Bandung conference, he made several useful interventions to ensure that it proceeded smoothly, but was not otherwise especially prominent.

He had become prime minister of Burma after the assassination of its first national leader, Aung San, in 1947, not long after Burma gained independence. He remained so for 14 years until the army seized power under General Ne Win in 1962, turning the country into the hermit dictatorship it has remained under ever since. Under U Nu, it had prospered moderately well, though modestly, backed by buoyant rice exports, on the basis of his 'Burmese

Way to Socialism', an eclectic amalgam of Buddhist and Marxist doctrines. U Nu's main aim was to avoid the evils of colonial capitalism. But the problems of maintaining national unity in a country of extremely diverse ethnic groups and local interests proved to be beyond the capabilities of U Nu and the AFPFL (Anti-Fascist Peoples Liberation League), which he headed. Ever since the army took over, national unity has been maintained by very un-Buddhist force. U Nu was imprisoned for some years and never again played a prominent political role.

In his autobiography, *Saturday's Son*, U Nu has astonishingly little to say about the Bandung conference, except that, 'Overall, the speeches…and communiqués were not of absorbing interest', although he found some value in it because 'the delegates got to know each other and to establish lasting friendships'. The relationship he established with Zhou Enlai seems to have been a particularly cordial one.

of bringing China into the wider world. On 25 September, the two men issued a joint statement that such a conference would be desirable and should be held soon. On his way home, Ali called in at Rangoon to discuss the idea with U Nu, who was supportive. The two others of the Colombo Five also agreed to the proposal to meet in Bogor in December to work out whether or how such a meeting should be organised.

The Bogor Conference, 28–30 December

The Bogor Conference put it all on track. By then, all of the Colombo Five were agreed on the desirability of an AA meeting. 'How different were the opinions expressed in the Bogor Conference than those at Colombo several months before', remarked Roeslan Abdulgani of their opening speeches. The broad aims of the conference were quickly decided upon, then various administrative matters about a conference secretariat (left mainly to Indonesia, with some representation and sharing of costs by the other four countries) and who would be regarded as sponsors. But other questions, particularly that of who should be invited, proved contentious and difficult.

It was quickly agreed in principle that invitations should go to all Asian and African countries that were independent or self-governing, with the proviso that acceptance 'in no way involves or even implies any change in the status of that country or its relationship with others' whom it did not recognise officially. Acceptance implied only that the country invited 'was in general agreement with the purposes of the conference'. Indonesia reported that 14 countries had already been sounded out and had accepted, but Thailand and the Philippines, both members of SEATO, had not yet replied. The discussion then turned to the 'borderline cases' over which far greater difficulties arose.

Israel posed the first problem because of the risk that if she were to attend, the Arab countries would probably refuse. Burma and Ceylon

MOHAMMED ALI BOGRA (1909–1963)

Mohammed Ali Bogra had been prime minister of Pakistan for two years before the Bandung conference, at a time of mounting political turbulence during the years after the death of the legendary M.A. Jinnah, the 'founder of Pakistan'. Ali came of a family prominent in Bengali politics, his grandfather having been the first Muslim to become a minister in the Bengal government under the British. After graduating from the University of Calcutta, Ali held a series of local administrative positions. He was elected to the Bengal Legislative Council at the youthful age of 28, then became a parliamentary secretary and in 1946 a minister in

the government of Bengal before partition. (The contrast with Nehru's career to that point, or Sukarno's, could hardly have been greater.) He became a member of Pakistan's Constituent Assembly after independence, but was appointed ambassador to Burma soon after, then to Canada and later the US, before being recalled to be prime minister of Pakistan in 1953.

At Bandung (and in the meetings of the Colombo Five preceding it), he was constantly at odds with Nehru and one of the strongest defenders of pro-US collective security pacts. But his anti-communism had limits, for in private talks with Zhou Enlai he paved the way for the close alignment that developed between Pakistan and China over the following decade.

He ceased to be prime minister in 1955 and faded into political obscurity thereafter.

were vaguely in favour of Israel's participation, but Pakistan and Indonesia were opposed, and India, without opposing, took the view that the risk of the Arabs not attending if Israel were invited made it impolitic to do so. Hence it was agreed not to invite her. Agreement was easily reached about inviting Nepal, Turkey, Japan, the four states of Indochina, and two 'half-independent' countries which were already self-governing, Sudan and the Gold Coast (later to be known as Ghana). The Central African Federation ('white' Southern Rhodesia, plus Zambia and Nyasaland) was proposed by India, partly on the ground that there were large numbers of Indians there, and partly to make the point that no racial or colour prejudice should be manifest. After some objections were dismissed, it was decided to send an invitation (which was duly refused by the white supremacist government of that time). South Africa, however, with its white, blatantly racist apartheid regime, was simply not invited.

The question of an invitation to China—or to Taiwan?—aroused the major debate. U Nu ruled out any serious thought of inviting Taiwan by stating flatly that if that happened Burma would withdraw as a sponsor. And since he had earlier given way on the question of Israel, he got his way here. But Mohammed Ali of Pakistan raised an objection that if China were invited, Thailand and the Philippines, the other Asian SEATO members, might refuse. U Nu replied that a conference of Asian nations without China would have no credibility, so he would refuse to attend if China were not there. Mohammed Ali did not persist with his case.

It was decided not to invite either North or South Korea, since political difficulties over their legal status posed insuperable problems, pending a peace treaty to end the Korean war. On the other hand, both communist North Vietnam and the anti-communist 'State of Vietnam' (South), which had been recognised in the Geneva Accords, were invited—and both came. So a final list of 30 participants was agreed upon, with the invitations to be issued by Indonesia.

The venue of the conference was to be left to the prime minister of Indonesia, it was agreed. 'I decided on Bandung', says Ali (although Roeslan Abdulgani says that the choice was actually made by Sukarno, who had spent his student days and an early, happy marriage there). The main reason for preferring Bandung to Jakarta, the national capital, seems to have been the difficulty of ensuring adequate accommodation there, since Jakarta had few large hotels and an inflexible rental market—quite the reverse of the present-day situation. And Bandung was a much cooler, more spacious city than hot, overcrowded Jakarta, an important consideration in the days when air-conditioning was almost unknown in Indonesia except in wealthy Western houses and offices.

From Bogor to Bandung

The invitations were sent out in January, with most acceptances following soon after. But Thailand and the Philippines were sluggish about replying, rumoured to be awaiting a clear signal from Washington before making a decision. (Washington ultimately shifted from an initial attitude of disdain for the very idea of the conference to one of urging the anti-communists to go in order to counter the influence of India and China.) Nasser did not make up his mind until Nehru visited him in February to persuade him to attend. Other Arabs were initially not enthusiastic, but decided to come in order to resist the influence of both the communist bloc and the neutralists. The Central African Federation was ultimately the only country to decline its invitation.

The numerical disparity between the only six African countries and 23 Asian or Middle Eastern ones was very blatant, but reflected the fact that only Egypt, Ethiopia, Liberia and Libya were yet independent there, and only Sudan and the Gold Coast (Ghana) close to it. (Sudan had not even designed its own flag at that time, so the conference organisers ingeniously resolved a protocol problem by flying a plain flag for them with the word 'SUDAN' printed across it!) The independence struggles of the French colonies in North Africa—Algeria, Morocco and Tunisia—provoked much comment at the conference, but the other colonies of Central and Southern Africa drew very little. The most obvious Asian absentees, apart from North and South Korea, were Malaya and Singapore, which were not yet clearly within sight of obtaining independence. But Indonesia unofficially encouraged a Malayan nationalist leader, Dr Burhanuddin, to attend as an observer.

There were some minor disagreements within the five-nation advisory body between the Indian representative and the Indonesians, which led to the former resigning and returning to India—not a good omen. But the preparatory arrangements in Bandung proceeded well after the very competent Roeslan Abdulgani took charge there personally in early 1955.

The two conference buildings, the Gedung Merdeka (the former Dutch social club Concordia), and a large government office building several kilometres to the north renamed 'Gedung Dwi-warna' ('Two-coloured'—the name frequently used to refer to the Indonesian national

flag, the 'Red and White'), were reconditioned and the big ballroom of the former converted into a suitable hall for the large open sessions. The closed committee sessions took place in the Gedung Dwi-warna. The larger, modern hotels nearby, the Savoy Homann, the Grand Hotel Preanger ('that obscene symbol of Dutch colonialism', according to Legge) and several others, were taken over for the delegations. In addition, a number of large Dutch bungalows along the main roads running north towards the hills around Ciumbuleuit and Lembang, just beyond Bandung, were rented for the heads of delegations. An Islamic hotel near the main mosque was reserved for journalists, most of whom had to share rooms as there were about 700 covering the conference—300 from Indonesia and 400 from elsewhere. There were 30 from Thailand alone (most of them rumoured to be SEATO agents, according to Ali Sastroamidjojo!) and 70 from the US. Altogether, Bandung was transformed for and by the conference.

A large Indonesian delegation attended the conference, almost twice as large as any other, led by the Foreign Minister, Mr Sunario, in

The Colombo Five prime ministers at the Bogor Conference.

addition to the conference chairman, Ali Sastroamidjojo, the secretary, Roeslan Abdulgani, and, for the opening ceremonies only, President Sukarno. It included a former foreign minister, Ahmad Subardjo, Information Minister Dr H. Lumban Tobing, Education and Culture Minister Mohammad Yamin, and some other distinguished citizens.

An awkward problem of timing arose. It had been agreed at Bogor that the conference would be held in the last week of April. But it was later realised that the Muslim fasting month, Ramadan, was due to begin on 24 April. It was estimated that 10 days before that would be needed for the conference. Then it was found that owing to a Buddhist holy day, the delegates from Burma and Thailand would not be able to set out before 15 April. So, 'caught in a pinch between the Sacred Days of Buddhism and Islam', Roeslan Abdulgani has written, the conference committee had to settle for a six-day conference between Monday, 18 April, and Saturday, 23 April. In the end, it had to be extended into the 24th to complete the agenda.

The crash of an Air India plane chartered to fly the Chinese delegation from Hong Kong to Jakarta on 11 April, in Indonesian waters near Natuna Island, caused some last minute trepidation, for it was feared at first that it may have been carrying Zhou Enlai. It turned out that Zhou was not on it, although some members of the Chinese delegation were and 10 of them were killed. Sabotage was suspected (inevitably, of the CIA or KMT) and security intensified as a result. But apart from that, and one or two minor worries, the conference turned out to be free of adverse security incidents.

The bustling Jalan Braga in the 1930s, regarded then as the smartest street in any Indonesian city.

Crowds waiting to greet conference delegates outside the Savoy Homann Hotel.

Several distinguished foreign visitors attended the conference with official status as observers, in addition to diplomatic representatives of other, non-participating countries: Archbishop Makarios of Cyprus, Adam Clayton Powell, a black American member of Congress, ex-communist writer Richard Wright, as well as Professor George Kahin, the foremost American scholar of Indonesian and Southeast Asian studies. There were even two unofficial Australians in attendance, John Burton and Professor C.P. Fitzgerald, who endeavoured to highlight their belief that Australia should have sought to be involved officially in any conference of Asian nations (a theme that Nehru welcomed in his concluding speech). And messages of support for the conference were sent by various foreign governments, including the Soviet Union—but conspicuously not the US—and by a group of distinguished Americans, including Pearl Buck and Lewis Mumford. The conference had caught the imagination of many people throughout the world by the time it opened.

AT BANDUNG: DRAMAS, DISPUTES, DECISIONS

Bandung greeted the delegates to the AA Conference in an atmosphere of extraordinary enthusiasm, friendliness and optimism as they began to arrive over the preceding weekend. Then and every morning throughout that week, there were large crowds milling on Jalan Asia-Afrika, around the conference building, Gedung Merdeka, or the Homann and Preanger Hotels, to watch and cheer the various delegates, many in colourful national dress, as they walked across to the conference building.

While the conference turned out to be a triumphant success, it veered close to deadlock and failure several times, most seriously at the eleventh hour, since consensus on all resolutions put forward was essential under the rules of procedure adopted. The gulf between the large group of Western-aligned nations, committed to collective security treaties such as SEATO or the Baghdad Pact, and the much smaller group espousing non-alignment (only India, Burma and Indonesia, essentially) seemed at times almost unbridgeable, despite all the expressions of unity and goodwill towards reaching consensus. The seeds of conflict between the two camps were clearly apparent in the opening speeches, when several pro-Western delegates attacked communism as a new form of colonialism and revealed their serious distrust for the idea of peaceful coexistence embodied in the Nehru–Zhou Enlai set of *Panch Shila* principles, which they saw as redolent of communist propaganda. In a conference committed to reaching consensus on the issues before it, the problems were formidable.

There were other doubts and uncertainties initially. Could the Indonesians, with so little experience of such large meetings, really handle the administrative and logistical problems inherent in so large a gathering? Many people—

Crowds waiting to catch a glimpse of the conference delegates along Jalan Asia-Afrika; the street was renamed for the conference.

some Indonesians as well as foreigners—were sceptical about that initially (although it turned out they were quite wrong). How would the Chinese delegation react to such an unfamiliar and perhaps unfriendly gathering? Could the differences between the pro-Western and non-aligned nations be bridged on the contentious issues on the agenda?

In retrospect, it is clear that the successful outcome was a combination of good luck and skilful management of the issues, thanks largely to the conciliatory stance of Zhou Enlai and the tact of the Indonesian organisers, along with Nehru's experience of such meetings to call upon when necessary. But Cold War issues certainly intruded into the conference halls of Bandung just as they clouded the international atmosphere right across the world, creating serious divisions among the various camps.

Yet there were really only two periods of serious tension and drama over the course of the week, the first on Thursday afternoon when Sir John Kotelawala caused a commotion with an attack on Soviet 'colonialism' in Eastern Europe (a matter which was quickly pushed into the background, at least temporarily), the second during some torrid

President Sukarno, Vice-President Hatta and other heads of state with their wives at the evening reception.

debates on military alliances and peaceful coexistence over the last three days. In the earlier part of the week, things actually proceeded fairly smoothly in the open plenary sessions, without any major clashes. One of the main highlights was Zhou Enlai's first speech on Tuesday, discussed below, at the conclusion of the various opening addresses.

A rift that developed between the Indian and Pakistani delegations on the first Sunday, even before the conference opened, cast an ominous shadow portending troubles ahead. As many delegations had already arrived at Bandung by Sunday morning, Nehru suggested that it would be useful to have an informal meeting immediately of the heads of delegations already there, in order to save time in an already truncated conference by working out the most suitable rules of procedure. This was done—consensus rather than voting being preferred—and a sensible suggestion he made that the opening speeches be merely tabled rather than read out in full, was informally adopted. But this had an unfortunate consequence, for the Pakistani delegation had not yet arrived, and as soon as Mohammed Ali heard about it, he 'exploded' in anger, according to Roeslan Abdulgani, charging that as one of the five sponsors of the conference, Pakistan should have been represented at any such meeting. Nehru was trying to

Indira Gandhi (1917–1984), Nehru's daughter and assistant at the conference.

WOMEN AT BANDUNG

There were no women delegates. The only delegation to have any women listed was the very large Indonesian one, with Mrs Mariah Ulfah Santoso, a former cabinet minister and later cabinet secretary, and Mrs Pudjobuntoro of the West Irian Bureau.

Indira Gandhi accompanied her father, Jawaharlal Nehru, as an assistant and sometimes hostess (his wife having died nearly 20 years before), but she was not listed in the Indian delegation. Of all the women and men attending the conference, she was to rise to greatest heights, as prime minister of India from 1966 to 1977 and 1980 to 1984, when she was assassinated.

THE DELEGATION HEADS: NATIONALISTS, ARISTOCRATS AND BUREAUCRATS

The heads of delegations were a diverse lot. About half a dozen of them had strong nationalist credentials and were widely known internationally, e.g. Nehru, Zhou Enlai, Sukarno, U Nu, Nasser, Pham Van Dong and Ali Sastroamidjojo. (The two communists had fought long and hard in their countries' nationalist struggles and shared much of the same ideology, but were not close friends after Pham felt he had been 'double-crossed'—his own words—by Zhou at Geneva.) Then there were four quasi-nationalists of a distinctly less strong variety: Sir John Kotelawala of Ceylon, Mohammed Ali of Pakistan, 'General' Romulo of the Philippines (who would no doubt have preferred to believe he belonged in the first group), and Kojo Botsio of the Gold Coast, filling in for the much better known African nationalist Kwame Nkrumah, who was too involved with preparations for Ghana's imminent independence to make it to Bandung. Several of the delegates might even have been classed as 'lackeys of the imperialists', in less favourable circumstances.

There was a handful of men from old, feudalistic families (no women, of course) who held high office in their lands for that reason: most notably Prince Faisal of Saudi Arabia (later to become king), Prince Wan Waithayakon, an old and wise counsellor to his country's rulers, Prince Norodom Sihanouk, who had only recently abdicated the throne of Cambodia in favour of his father, after nearly 14 years as king, the Emir Seifal al-Islam al-Hassan of Yemen, Sayed Ismail el-Azhari, grandson of a former Grand Mufti of Sudan.

Then there was a large and varied group of men with backgrounds in diplomacy, law, politics or the bureaucracy, who cannot easily be fitted into any of the above categories: Dr Mohammed Fadhil Jamali of Iraq, Dr Jalal Abdoh of Iran, Takasaki of Japan, Sami Bek Solh of Lebanon and Fatin Rustu Zorlu of Turkey, who were all quite prominent at the conference. Others were the little known representatives of Afghanistan, Ethiopia, Jordan, Laos, Liberia, Libya, Laos, Nepal, Syria and the State of Vietnam, who did not have much to say there at all.

Most of them were men in or near their 40s, with half a dozen in their 50s. Only Prince Wan (aged 65), Nehru (66), Takasaki (70) and three others were over 60. Nasser, at 37, was one of the youngest there.

OTHER DELEGATES

AFGHANISTAN

MOHAMMAD NAIM (1911–1978)
MINISTER FOR FOREIGN AFFAIRS AND DEPUTY PRIME MINISTER.

He held various diplomatic posts in Rome, London and Washington.

ETHIOPIA

YILMA DERESSA (1907–1979)
CHAIR OF ETHIOPIA'S DELEGATION TO THE UN.

Educated at Victoria College, Alexandria, and the London School of Economics. Ethiopian ambassador to Washington from 1953 to 1955. Previously was secretary-general, Ministry of Foreign Affairs, 1941, and minister of commerce and industry, 1949.

GOLD COAST

KOJO BOTSIO (1916–2001)
MINISTER OF STATE AND MEMBER OF LEGISLATIVE ASSEMBLY.

Educated in Freetown, then at Oxford in Education, became vice-principal of the state college in Gold Coast from 1947 to 1949 and newspaper editor. Imprisoned briefly for political activities. Elected to Legislative Assembly and appointed minister of education and social welfare. Served as minister in Nkrumah's second cabinet. Stood in for Nkrumah at Bandung.

JORDAN

HUZA EL-MAJALI (1916–1960)
MINISTER OF JUSTICE.

Educated in Jordan, then at the Faculty of Law, Damascus. Was a barrister till 1946, then mayor of Amman from 1946 to 1949, member of Parliament in 1949, and minister of justice in 1950. He was mainly concerned at the conference with Israel and the plight of the Palestinean Arabs.

LEBANON

SAMI BEK SOLH (1890–1968)
PRIME MINISTER OF LEBANON.

One of the most experienced and cosmopolitan delegates at Bandung, he was educated at primary school in Istanbul in two languages, Turkish and French; secondary and tertiary education (Law) in Beirut and Istanbul. He worked in the Ministry of Justice as director of communications, Baghdad; inspector-general of railways in Anatolia (Turkey); lawyer at the Court of Appeal, Beirut, then attorney-general and president of the Supreme Court. He was a member of Parliament and prime minister on several occasions between 1942 and 1958. His deputy at Bandung was the young Charles Malik, Lebanon's ambassador to the US and one of the authors of the UN Declaration of Human Rights, a very able diplomat.

LIBERIA

MOMOLU DUKULY (1903–*unknown*)

Educated at the College of West Africa. Was a government official in the 1920s, and was called to the Bar in 1928. From 1928, he served as assistant secretary of state and ambassador to Haiti and Costa Rica. Was the acting secretary of state in 1954.

LIBYA

MAHMOUD MUNTASSER (1930–1970)

Having attended military school in Italy, then the University of Rome, he was vice-chairman of the National Administrative council under British military administration during WWII, and held various administrative and political positions after Libya became independent in December 1951. In 1954, he was ambassador to the UK.

PAL

or-General SOVAG JUNG THAPA (1910–*unknown*)

Educated in Nepal, Calcutta and Bangalore. Became Nepal's government representative in India in 1930. Member of the first Nepalese mission to London, 1930, and was a military attaché there till 1937. Served as member of Parliament in 1950 and defence secretary from 1951 to 1954.

JDI ARABIA

H the Emir FAISAL IBN ABDUL AZIZ AL-SAUD (1906–1975)
MINISTER FOR FOREIGN AFFAIRS, SAUDI ARABIA; PRESIDENT OF THE COUNCIL OF MINISTERS; LATER KING OF SAUDI ARABIA 1964–75.

Son of King Abdul Aziz Abdul Rachman al-Saud, he was a warrior, strong administrator and diplomat. He fought his first battle in the field in 1921; was the commander of his father's victorious army which united the Kingdom of Hejaz with the Sultanate of Nejd in 1935; was vice-roy of Hejaz in 1927. He was appointed minister for foreign affairs, and attended many international conferences before, during and after World War II, including the San Francisco UN Conference of 1945; he was frequently the chairman of the Saudi delegation to the UN. After the death of his father in November 1953, his elder brother was proclaimed King Saud I of Saudi Arabia, with Faisal named successor to the throne. Prime minister from 1954, effective power was transferred to him by Saud in 1962 in order to deal with economic problems. He became king on Saud's death two years later. A strong and relatively enlightened leader, although he retained absolute power. He was murdered by a nephew in 1975.

STATE OF VIETNAM

NGUYEN VAN THOAI (*unknown*)
MINISTER FOR PLANNING AND RECONSTRUCTION (IN THE DIEM CABINET).

Educated in Paris, attained Doctor of Chemistry in 1944. Was a professor of Chemistry at the University of Paris until his return to Vietnam.

SUDAN

SAYED ISMAIL EL-AZHARI (1900–1969)
PRIME MINISTER OF SUDAN 1954–8.

Educated at Gordon Memorial College, Khartoum and the American University, Beirut. Leader of a radical group of pro-Egypt students in the 1940s, who formed Sudan's first real political party in 1951. He won the 1953 elections easily and became the first prime minister until displaced by a military coup in 1958. Later was president of the Supreme Council of Sudan from 1964 to 1968, before again overthrown by a coup. He died soon after.

SYRIA

KHALED EL-AZM (1903–1965)
FOREIGN MINISTER FOR FOREIGN AFFAIRS, 1955.

Educated at Law College, Damascus. He was Chief of Government in 1941 (under the French), and Deputy for Damascus in 1943. He was not prominent in the Bandung debates.

YEMEN

HRH the Emir SEIF AL-ISLAM AL-HASSAN (1907–*unknown*)
PRIME MINISTER OF YEMEN.

Brother of the king of Yemen, he held high posts in the government service as minister of war, president of the Council of Ministers, and minister of interior.

The main assembly hall of the conference was in the Gedung Merdeka.

'patronise' and dominate the other delegates, he claimed at a hastily convened meeting of the five sponsors, waving his finger at Nehru aggressively. He even refused to abide by the proposal to table the opening addresses. Several others followed him on that, which meant that most of the Monday and Tuesday open sessions were taken up with fairly predictable speeches.

President Sukarno's opening address

Sukarno's opening address on Monday morning, in his characteristically high-flown style, set the tone the Indonesians would have expected of him for such an occasion.

> I am proud that my country is your host. But my thoughts are not wholly of the honour that is Indonesia's today. No. My mind is darkened by other considerations… You have not gathered together in a world of peace and unity and cooperation. Great chasms yawn between nations and groups of nations. Our unhappy world is torn and tortured, and the peoples of all countries walk in fear lest the dogs of war are unchained once again.

He went on to tell how in a previous speech he had referred to the 'Lifeline of Imperialism' that used to run from the Mediterranean through the Suez Canal and the Indian Ocean to the South China Sea and the Sea of Japan, alongside which 'the territories on both sides of this lifeline were colonies, the peoples were unfree, their futures mortgaged to an alien system'.

One cannot overstress the fact that economic difficulties may well lead to acceptance of conditional foreign assistance which could be a real menace to national freedom and sovereignty...
— Sudan's delegate

Along that lifeline was pumped the lifeblood of colonialism... And today in this hall are gathered together the leaders of those same peoples. They are no longer the victims of colonialism... You are representatives of free peoples, peoples of a different stature and standing in the world... Nations, States have awoken from a sleep of centuries. The passive peoples have gone, the outward tranquility has made place for struggle and activity. Irresistible forces have swept the two continents... Hurricanes of national awakening and reawakening have swept over the land, shaking it, changing it, changing it for the better.

He said much more about colonialism.

How is it possible for us to be disinterested about colonialism? For us, colonialism is not something far and distant. We have known it in all its ruthlessness... But we should not think of it as something that is dead, nor only in the classic form we all know... Colonialism also has its modern dress, in the form of economic control, intellectual control, actual physical control by a small but determined minority with a nation. It is a skilful and determined enemy... Colonialism is an evil thing, and one which must be eradicated from the earth.

Turning to the urgent question of preserving peace, he asked:

What can we do? The peoples of Asia and Africa wield little physical power. Even their economic strength is dispersed and slight. We cannot indulge in power politics... [But] we can do much. We can inject the voice of reason into world affairs. We can mobilise all the spiritual, all the moral, all the political strength of Asia and Africa on the side of peace. We, the peoples of Asia and Africa, 1,400 million strong, far more than half the human population of the world, we can mobilise what I have called the 'Moral Violence of Nations' in favour of peace. We can demonstrate to the minority of the world which lives on the other continents...that whatever strength we have will always be thrown on the side of peace.

Fine words (though they might have returned to mock him a decade later, when Indonesia used armed force against Malaysia in the course of its *Konfrontasi* policy). 'All of us are united,' Sukarno declared, 'by more important things than those which superficially divide us.'

The Gedung Dwi-warna was the venue for the closed sessions of the Political Committee (and other committees) throughout the conference.

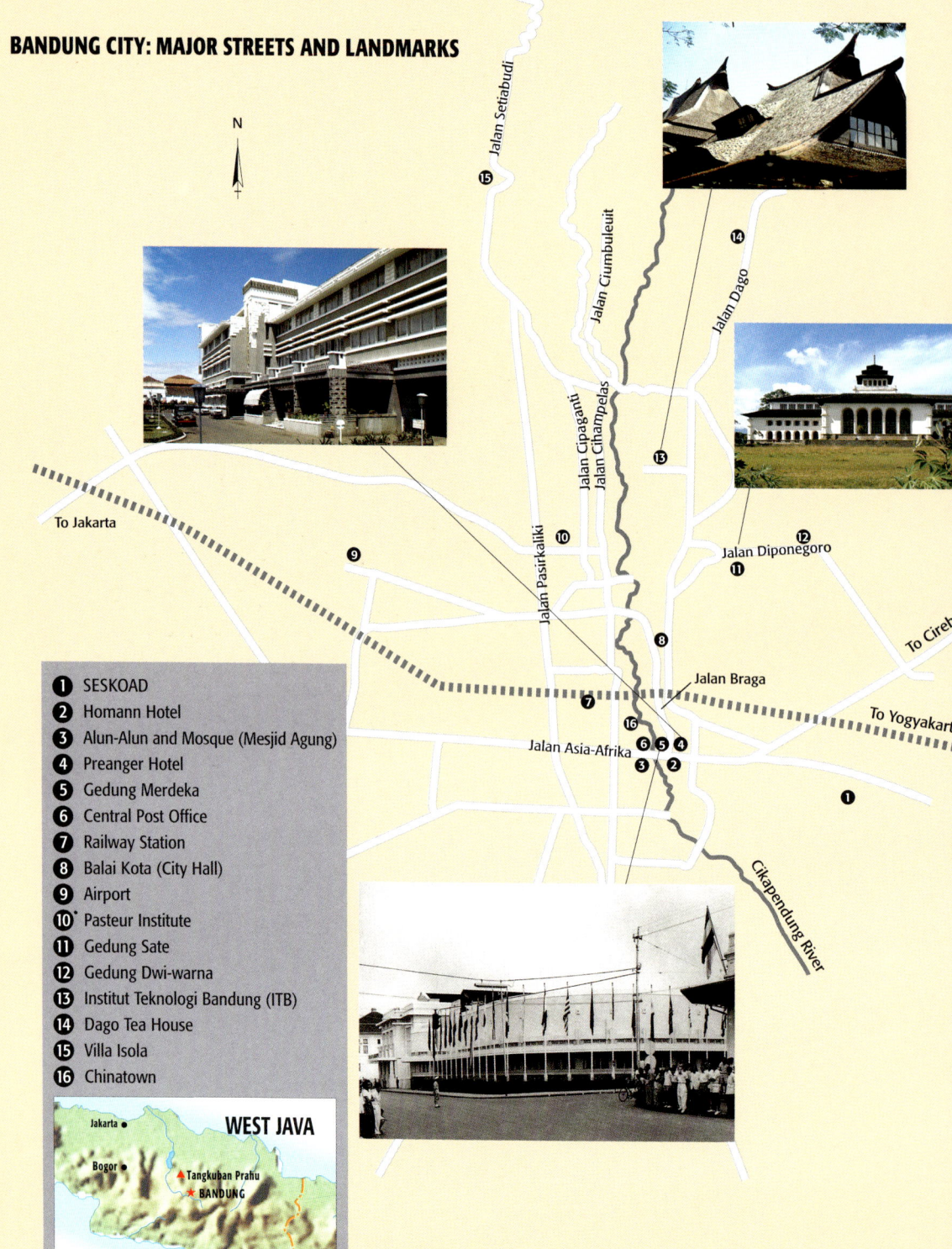

BANDUNG CITY: MAJOR STREETS AND LANDMARKS

N

To Lembang

Jalan Setiabudi

Jalan Ciumbuleuit

Jalan Dago

Jalan Cipaganti

Jalan Cihampelas

Jalan Pasirkaliki

To Jakarta

Jalan Diponegoro

To Cirebo

Jalan Braga

To Yogyakarta

Jalan Asia-Afrika

Cikapendung River

1. SESKOAD
2. Homann Hotel
3. Alun-Alun and Mosque (Mesjid Agung)
4. Preanger Hotel
5. Gedung Merdeka
6. Central Post Office
7. Railway Station
8. Balai Kota (City Hall)
9. Airport
10. Pasteur Institute
11. Gedung Sate
12. Gedung Dwi-warna
13. Institut Teknologi Bandung (ITB)
14. Dago Tea House
15. Villa Isola
16. Chinatown

WEST JAVA

Jakarta

Bogor

Tangkuban Prahu

BANDUNG

CARLOS P. ROMULO (1899–1985)

'Versatile Chief Delegate from the Philippines, General Romulo' (as the conference *Who's Who* rather lavishly described him—modesty was never his strong suit) was the most voluble and pro-Western delegate at the conference, yet also a great exponent of nationalist, anti-colonialist and anti-racialist rhetoric. That must have required some mental juggling in 1955, only a few months after the Manila Conference had given rise to the formation of SEATO, amidst copious Dullesian rhetoric about the 'evils' of communism. But Romulo never displayed any lack of self-assurance on such matters.

His anti-colonialist rhetoric was often quite remote from the political realities of his country's close alignment with and economic subordination to the US. He had no hesitation in talking effusively about 'a foreign policy of closer cooperation with our Asian neighbours, of regionalism and more intense dealings with them [which] bears directly on our primordial goal of nationhood and sense of identity'.

He had earlier been aide de camp to General MacArthur on Corregidor in early 1942, and had accompanied him and Manuel Quezon, the leading Filipino politician, in their flight to Australia and then Washington after the Japanese overran Luzon. He acted as information attaché to Quezon (and to President Osmeña after Quezon's death) until they returned to the Philippines in October 1944. (Romulo figures prominently alongside them both in the carefully staged official photographs of them striding through the surf at Leyte just before MacArthur's 'I have returned' statement to the Filipino people.) Romulo was given the rank of Lieutenant Colonel at the time of that adventure and later had it ratcheted up to General, which was how he preferred to be known. He also received many honorary degrees in later life and a Pulitzer Prize in 1941. His writings and speeches were copious, his book titles usually colourful.

Romulo was secretary for foreign affairs in 1950–52, 1968–70 and 1978–84 (the latter two terms were under President Marcos) and secretary for education in 1966–8. He was periodically head of the Philippines mission to the UN between 1945 and 1953 (and president of the General Assembly in 1949–50), as well as ambassador to Washington from 1952 to 1956. It could not be said he was inexperienced in international affairs. But as his 1956 book on *The Meaning of Bandung* reveals, his enthusiasm for Afro-Asian solidarity and the 'spirit of Bandung' was not altogether convincing.

> We are united, for instance, by a common detestation of colonialism in whatever form it appears. We are united by a common detestation of racialism. We are united by a common determination to preserve and stabilise peace in the world…

Sukarno's speech was greeted by enthusiastic applause and warm praise by many, including Nehru. As Ali Sastroamidjojo was to describe it years later, Sukarno was able to fascinate and enthral the audience for a whole hour, despite speaking in English, which was a foreign language to him.

Sukarno did not play any further part in the conference, however,

[T]here are three international forces in the world today that disturb peace and harmony… The first is what we might call old-time colonialism which has been gradually crumbling since the end of World War I. The fact that most of us here are new countries…is a proof of the passing away of old-time colonialism… The second disturbing force is that of Zionism… certainly the last chapter in the book of old colonialism. It is one of the blackest and darkest chapters in human history. It is the worst offspring of imperialism… The third force that is causing unrest in the world at large today is communism. Communism is a one-sided materialistic religion. It denies God and the spiritual heritage of mankind… It breeds hatred amongst classes and peoples… [It confronts] the world with a new form of colonialism, much deadlier than the old one. Today the communist world has subjected races in Asia and Eastern Europe on a much larger scale than any old colonial power. Just think of the vast areas of Turkistan… of the fate of Estonia, Latvia and Lithuania… of Poland, Romania and Czechoslovakia after the Second World War. Under the old form of colonialism there is some chance of one hearing the cries of pain of the subjugated peoples. Under communist domination, however, no such cries are permitted to be heard.

– Iraqi delegate

DR MOHAMMAD FADHIL JAMALI (1903–1997)
HEAD OF IRAQ'S MISSION TO THE UN

The leader of Iraq's delegation, Dr Mohammad Fadhil Jamali, was also a member of his country's Parliament and a distinguished educationalist, with degrees from the American University in Beirut and a PhD from Columbia. He had twice been prime minister (under the British-backed regime of Nuri Es-Said) and foreign minister six times, including being Iraq's signatory to the UN Charter in 1945. Roeslan Abdulgani describes him as adamantly anti-communist and opposed to the Soviet Union, but appeared to have some admiration for him. After the 1958 overthrow of Nuri Es-Said's government by a Baathist military coup, he was sentenced to death. The sentence was later commuted to life imprisonment, during which he composed *Letters on Islam, Written by a Father in Prison to his Son*.

ALI AMINI (1905–1992)
MINISTER OF FINANCE; LEADER OF THE IRANIAN DELEGATION

Ali Amini was Iran's minister of finance in 1955, and later became prime minister for a short time in the 1960s as a moderate reformer (with US backing) in the government of Shah Reza Pahlavi. He was leader of the Iranian delegation to the Bandung conference, but appears to have left much of the speech-making to his deputy, Dr Jalal Abdoh, Iran's permanent representative to the UN and an experienced diplomat. While clearly anti-communist, they were less strongly so than their Iraqi and Turkish colleagues.

returning to Bogor and leaving the field clear for his prime minister, foreign minister and others. But he had helped establish a mood which was to prevail throughout, despite the wrangles that developed later.

The speeches that followed over the next two days contained few surprises, although there were some interesting nuances here and there. The first speaker to allude to 'the new colonialism of the Soviet Union' was Jalal Abdoh (Iran's permanent representative at the UN), in very indirect terms; then Dr Mohammad Jamali of Iraq did so quite bluntly, as also did Fatin Rustu Zorlu of Turkey and Carlos Romulo of the Philippines. They all steered clear of any mention of China, however, in their condemnations. Prince Sihanouk of Cambodia raised other concerns about China, although gently and indirectly, followed in much the same vein by the prime minister of Laos, Katay Don Sasorith, and Prince Wan of Thailand. Prime Minister Mohammed Ali of Pakistan, who was highly sceptical about peaceful coexistence, advanced his view that the Five Principles advocated by Nehru and Zhou needed to be supplemented by two other principles to become the 'Seven Pillars of Peace', an issue we will encounter in a later debate. Roeslan Abdulgani later commented that Mohammed Ali's aim was 'to obtain justification and formal legalisation in the AA Conference that would justify their membership of SEATO, and to press India into accepting a plebiscite in Kashmir'.

Zhou Enlai's first speech

At the end of the second day of rather turgid opening speeches, Zhou Enlai made an off-the-cuff intervention to supplement the written address China had tabled, because he felt it necessary to answer some of the points already raised. China had come to Bandung

> to seek unity and not to quarrel... [T]o seek common ground and not to create divergences.

He had not brought up issues of concern to China such as the

THE ZHOU ENLAI-SUNARIO AGREEMENT ON DUAL NATIONALITY

The signing of an agreement on Dual Nationality between China and Indonesia during the course of the Bandung conference was an astute piece of international politics on Zhou's part and a useful feather in the cap for the Ali Sastroamidjojo government. Substantively it represented the first ever public statement by the Chinese government of its willingness to allow the overseas Chinese living in Southeast Asian countries to opt for the nationality of that country if they wished.

It marked an abandonment of the long-held principle of *ius sanguinis* as the basis for Chinese nationality (i.e. by descent), under which all persons born of a Chinese father or mother—the latter in cases where the nationality of the father was unknown—were held to be Chinese nationals. That principle had been laid down in the Qing dynasty nationality law of 1909 and maintained by both the KMT regime and the PRC. But when the newly independent countries of Southeast Asia began to draft their own nationality laws in the 1950s, with a preference for the *ius soli* principle (i.e. that anyone born in that country was entitled to become a citizen of it), the Chinese claim upon the loyalty of all ethnic Chinese by virtue of their descent could only be reconciled with the new approach if it was

accepted that their ethnic Chinese citizens might also hold dual nationalities. Many Southeast Asians objected to that assumption, although none of the governments of the region had made any progress towards resolving the issue with China until the Indonesians did so at Bandung. Hence Zhou's concession that ethnic Chinese might adopt Indonesian nationality (or any other), and his admonition to the Chinese overseas that it would be best if they complied with the laws and customs of their adopted country, was a major step towards the ultimate resolution of that problem.

It was not the final step, however, even in relation to Indonesia's tortuous progress towards devising a nationality law that would resolve the issue. That was not achieved until 1962 after some bitter wrangling—and was later repudiated in 1967 when other disputes arose. For the other countries of Southeast Asia, none of whom followed the Indonesian path of negotiating a solution with China bilaterally, various aspects of the problem still remained unsettled even in the 1980s. But they were certainly heartened by Zhou's willingness to drop the *ius sanguinis* principle, which underlined the generally cordial approach he was taking towards his neighbours on other issues at Bandung.

Taiwan issue or China's exclusion from the UN because they would have caused the conference to be 'dragged into disputes about all these problems without any solution'. The conference should

> seek common ground among us, while keeping our differences… None of us is asked to give up his own views, because difference in viewpoints is an objective reality.

After this conciliatory start, he went on to make four points that today seem unremarkable today but in 1955 were not. He urged that differences of ideology need not exclude us from one another. He acknowledged that, 'We communists are atheists, but we respect all who have religious beliefs' (and in his delegation was 'a pious imam of the Islamic faith' to testify to the PRC's religious tolerance). He tried to reassure his Southeast Asian neighbours that China had no aggressive or subversive designs upon them, highlighting the point with an assurance of his government's willingness to resolve the vexed legal issue of dual nationality of the ethnic Chinese citizens of the newly independent Southeast Asian nations (on which he signed a landmark Dual National-ity Agreement with Indonesia two days later). And he put great stress on the *Panch Shila*, the Five Principles of peaceful coexistence he had negotiated earlier with India, as the basis for normalisation of diplomatic relations with all Asian and African countries.

Zhou's speech made a powerful impression, with most commentators agreeing with Roeslan Abdulgani's description of his tone as 'modest and attractive'. And he showed this attitude not only in the open sessions but also 'in the closed sittings, in every dinner party, every reception and in the lobbies'. Even delegations which had previously been suspicious of him were impressed by his cordiality.

On Wednesday, the conference divided into three committees meeting in closed sessions in the Dwi-warna Building. The Political Committee, made up of heads of delegations, was charged with the most

THE WEST IRIAN ISSUE AT BANDUNG

For Indonesians, the West Irian issue was one of the most important items on the Bandung agenda, for they wanted to muster as much support as they could for their claim to the region when it was to be next raised in the UN General Assembly. It was not, as sometimes alleged, their main reason for promoting the Bandung conference, but it was certainly an important issue for Ali Sastroamidjojo's government.

The basis of the Indonesian claim was simply that West Irian (West New Guinea) had long been regarded internationally as an integral part of the Netherlands Indies, to which Indonesia was the successor state under the terms of the 1949 Dutch-Indonesian agreement on the transfer of sovereignty. But the Dutch had insisted on excluding West New Guinea for tangled reasons of domestic politics and national pride, so a compromise proposal to leave its status unresolved pending further discussions over the following 12 months was adopted in order to enable the more important aspects of Indonesia's independence to be resolved. Those negotiations soon became deadlocked, however, due to intransigence on both sides. So the Dutch remained in control of the region and there was little Indonesia could do about it, except try to mobilise international pressure against them. Hence the decision to take the issue to the UN in 1954 and later years. But although Indonesia won majority support in the General Assembly, it did not obtain the two-thirds majority deemed necessary under UN rules.

The issue arose at Bandung during the debate on colonialism, when Syria moved a motion (in effect on Indonesia's behalf, so that she did not appear to be pushing the issue too blatantly) that the Conference 'in the context of its expressed attitude on the abolition of colonialism… supported the position of Indonesia in the case of West Irian based on the relevant agreements between Indonesia and the Netherlands'. But it went on to express 'regret' that the UN had failed to assist the parties to reach a peaceful settlement of the issue, which provoked a quite unexpected debate over the appropriateness of using such a word. A curiously unpredictable division between the delegations over that matter had to be resolved by referring it to a drafting committee, which finally agreed to avoid the word 'regrets' and adopt a 'less heavy' form of words to much the same effect, which was unanimously approved by the Political Committee.

The outcome was useful to Indonesia in helping to broaden support for her cause at the UN, although it did not prove sufficient to win a two-thirds majority in crucial votes in 1956 and 1957, or later in 1961 when many more newly independent states were members. On both occasions, Indonesia switched from diplomatic pressure on the Dutch to economic pressures and later a combination of military threats and political pressure through the US to help achieve the incorporation of West Irian into her national territory.

important and contentious issues. The committees on Economic Cooperation and Cultural Cooperation aroused relatively little attention from the large press corps looking eagerly for any signs of serious controversy to report. The committee on self-determination took longer than expected to agree on a resolution supporting Indonesia's claim to West Irian (West New Guinea), although they were divided more on a question of wording than on the substance of the claim. The discussions on human rights in the Political Committee on Wednesday were notable mainly for the fact that Zhou at first declined to agree on this issue because he had no direct knowledge of the Charter, a result of China not being a UN member; but the rest of the delegates were persuaded by two of the original participants in the drafting of the UN Charter of Human Rights, Charles Malik and Carlos Romulo, into giving support to their views on the subject (including, ultimately, Zhou).

Things proceeded smoothly enough until late on Thursday when the otherwise mild Buddhist, Sir John Kotelawala, conjured up a sudden storm out of a clear sky.

Sir John Kotelawala's 'bombshell'

During the discussion of colonialism, Sir John made an unexpected and very explicit attack on

> another form of colonialism… those satellite states under communist domination in Central and Eastern Europe; of Hungary, Romania, Bulgaria, Albania, Czechoslovakia, Latvia, Lithuania and Poland. Are not these colonies as much as the colonial territories in Africa or Asia? And if we are united in our opposition to colonialism, should it not be our duty openly to declare our opposition to Soviet colonialism as much as to Western imperialism?

While Sir John's words were not very different from those of the Iraqi and Turkish delegates in their opening speeches, they caused a much greater stir, arousing an immediate protest from Zhou, who

Sir John Kotelawala (second from left) and Zhou Enlai (second from right), parties to a fierce debate over 'Soviet colonialism'.

demanded a right to reply the next day after he had been able to examine a written text of the speech. 'I granted Zhou's request,' Ali Sastroamidjojo recounted. Aware that this episode could cause the conference to collapse in a deadlock, Ali Sastroamidjojo

> immediately closed the meeting in order to allow the tense atmosphere to cool down a little. But suddenly Nehru asked what agenda item Kotelawala's speech would be included under next day, his annoyance indicating that he did not want the discussion of the speech to be continued and he wanted me to propose excluding it from the agenda.
>
> But that would have meant denying Zhou a right of reply which I had already promised him. So I firmly stated that the speech would be included under the agenda item entitled 'independent nations'… But the Indian delegation was apparently determined to prevent a debate on the speech [whereas] the supporters of Kotelawala…vigorously defended him and urged that the speech be discussed as widely and fully as possible. To close the meeting in an atmosphere that had become so heated and tense would not be wise thing to do.

So a heated debate continued until 6.30 pm and the tensions continued to flare even after it ended. Zhou immediately went up to Sir John and asked him, 'What do you want, Sir John, by proposing a discussion of Soviet colonialism? Is it to provoke the Republic of China? To split us apart and make the Conference fail?'

To which Sir John replied:

> Why do you become angry because of my criticism of the Soviet? I did not touch at all upon the relations of the Soviet with China in that question… I mentioned only the relations of the Soviet Union with the countries of Eastern Europe. Why did you react so hurriedly and ask to speak tomorrow morning? If you had just kept quiet, nothing would have happened.

To which Zhou just smiled and said, 'Very well, I'll think about it till tomorrow morning.' He shook hands and left. Nehru then came up to Sir

We have all suffered from colonialist ambitions. Ethiopia was one of the few independent countries on the African continent. That did not prevent our having been faced constantly with the necessity of a fierce struggle to preserve our independence against imperialistic designs. That's why, with due regard to the legal provisions of the charter...I apply the expression 'colonialism' to include also those territories subjected to the trusteeship regime...
– Ethiopian delegate

Momolu Dukuly (far right) and colleagues

Gamal Abdel Nasser (centre) with the Egyptian delegation.

Kojo Botsio (left) stood in for Kwame Nkrumah at Bandung.

Supporting members of the Japanese delegation.

The Laotian delegation in a closed committee session.

Major–General Thapa (left) and a colleague.

Prime Minister Sami Bek Solh and colleagues, including Charles Malik (second from right).

Supporting members of the Iranian delegation in open public session.

Prime Minister el-Azhari (with glasses) and colleagues in open session.

Vice-President Pelaez (with microphone) of the Philippines in a committee session.

John and asked, 'Why did you do that, Sir John? Why did you not show me your speech before you gave it?' To which Sir John's reply was simply, 'Why should I? Do you show me yours before you give them?' (It was a point noted gleefully by the Indonesians, who were very sensitive to Nehru's often didactic and patronising attitudes to 'lesser breeds'.) Nehru too just smiled and laughed diplomatically as they all walked out together.

Ali Sastromidjojo says that as soon as Nehru had left, he brought Zhou and Sir John together and asked the latter what he had intended by his remarks and whether he proposed to put forward a motion on the subject the next morning. Sir John replied, 'I didn't mean anything by my speech. I only wanted to get it off my chest.' To which Zhou thanked him and replied with relief, 'Now we are friends, aren't we?' Zhou later consulted Ali about how best to handle the matter the next day, since others would probably continue to denounce 'Soviet colonialism'. Ali urged him just to follow the same line as in his opening speech on the Tuesday,

> which had been so well received. Later in the evening, senior diplomats from the Indonesian delegation held talks with the likely supporters of Sir John in an effort to persuade them to exercise restraint in the debate the next morning so as to avoid endangering the conference.

When the discussion was resumed in the Political Committee on Friday morning, the atmosphere was still tense but gradually began to relax. Before Zhou spoke, U Nu asked to speak on a point of order so as to appeal for restraint in any discussion of this 'new form of colonialism'. Sir John then made a brief statement repeating what he had said to Zhou in private on the previous evening and adding that as one of the conference sponsors he had no intention of creating difficulties or causing the conference to fail; so he would not put forward any resolution or motion on the subject. Zhou replied to Sir John's remarks about 'a new colonialism' as being an interpretation with which the Chinese delegation 'could not possibly agree'.

SUNARIO (1902–1997)

Foreign minister of Indonesia from August 1953 until July 1955, Sunario was leader of the Indonesian delegation at Bandung and a leading member of Indonesia's nationalist party, PNI, along with Ali Sastroamidjojo. They had both been among the first generation of young Dutch-educated pioneers of Indonesia's independence while studying law in Leiden in the 1920s, where Sunario was a secretary of the PPI, the first major nationalist students' group. Sunario became a strong advocate of 'unitary' rather than 'federal' Indonesia (which some Dutch officials and Dutch-leaning Indonesians were then advocating) and he continued his nationalist activities after his return to Indonesia in 1926. Working as a lawyer in Bandung, Jakarta, Medan and Makassar, he was also active in Sukarno's various nationalist parties, under close surveillance by the Dutch authorities.

After the proclamation of Indonesian independence in August 1945, Sunario became a member of the PNI and also of the KNIP (Indonesian National Committee) and its quasi-parliament, the Working Committee. As such, he later became a member of the first Provisional Parliament of the Republic after the transfer of sovereignty in late 1949. He became a leading figure in its Foreign Affairs section until he was appointed foreign minister in the Ali Sastroamidjojo cabinet.

In 1956, he became ambassador to Britain until 1961. After that, he returned to practise and teach law in Jakarta and Semarang, with a lower political profile. After the fall of Sukarno, he was appointed by General Suharto to the MPRS (Provisional Peoples' Consultative Assembly) from 1968 to 1971.

ROESLAN ABDULGANI (1914–)

Roeslan Abdulgani was elected secretary-general of the Bandung conference after serving as secretary of the Preparatory Committee which had made the arrangements for it over the preceding months. He was then secretary-general of the Indonesian Ministry of Foreign Affairs, having earlier been secretary-general of the Department of Information between 1947 and 1954.

He had previously begun to make a name for himself in Surabaya, his birthplace, at the time of the Battle for Surabaya in November 1945, during the early weeks of Indonesia's struggle for independence. Earlier in the 1930s, he was a leading figure in *Indonesia Muda*, the leading nationalist youth organisation in East Java. He eventually joined the PNI and became a prominent member of it.

He was politically very close to President Sukarno and served in various government posts under him during the 'Guided Democracy' years of 1959–65, particularly as the president's chief spokesman on ideological matters, which was his forte. The American writer Louis Fischer wrote that Roeslan was 'a brilliant conversationalist, well-read in current political literature and well-informed on world developments (a joy rarely encountered in Indonesia)'. He was minister for foreign affairs in 1956–7, and later became Indonesia's ambassador to the UN in the late 1960s under President Suharto.

He has written more copiously about the Bandung conference than any other Indonesian, and his 1981 book, *The Bandung Connection*, cited extensively here, is one of the most comprehensive accounts available.

> The peoples in the countries of Eastern Europe have selected their own system of government in accordance with their own will. One may like that system or may not: that is the freedom and right of everyone. But to put forward a new interpretation and have an argument about it will be of no help to this conference… The best way is to respect the views of each other and not enter into an argument about it [here] because it would not be fruitful and it would be impossible to reach any common understanding.

The debate continued throughout Friday morning, although the heat gradually went out of it. But Sir John's outburst had given rise to what became the most intense debate of the entire conference over the next two days, one which 'until the last threatened to produce a serious and disruptive deadlock'.

After Zhou's speech, Mohammed Ali argued that it was unrealistic to condemn French colonialism in Africa while ignoring that of the Soviet Union with its satellites in Eastern Europe. But he explicitly excluded China from his attack, saying that 'China is by no means an imperialist nation and she has no satellites'. He was supported by Iraq and Turkey, who introduced a motion condemning 'all types of

KATAY DON SASORITH (1904–1959)
PRIME MINISTER OF LAOS, 1954–6

One of the first of the few Lao nationalists in the 1940s, Katay—his forename, but the one he was most generally known by—was active in the *Lao Issarak* (Free Lao) movement in 1945 and became finance minister between 1951 and 1954, then prime minister, rather briefly. In the tangled Laotian politics of that time, dominated by the efforts of the French, Americans, Vietminh and Thais to exert influence in what was an exceptionally poor and vulnerable nation-in-making, he was an 'irrepressible' nationalist, an anti-communist and 'a consummate politician', as well as an enthusiastic writer on Lao history and literature.

At Bandung he had relatively little to say, in comparison with Sihanouk, Pham Van Dong and even Nguyen Van Thoai of South Vietnam. He later swung away from the neutralist-leaning politicians in Laos towards the Americans, becoming deputy prime minister and minister of defence in a right-wing government, until his early death in 1959.

*Where do we, the peoples of Asia and Africa,
stand: and for what do we stand in this world
dominated by fear?*
– Ali Sastroamidjojo, opening speech

colonialism, including international doctrines resorting to methods of force, infiltration and subversion'. This was supported by Iran, Japan, Lebanon, Liberia, Pakistan, the Philippines and Sudan. Nehru tried to salvage the situation by denying that the countries of Eastern Europe could be regarded as colonial since they were recognised as sovereign and independent by the UN and were therefore outside the scope of the conference agenda. But the anti-Soviet group was insistent; so in order that the committee could proceed to other matters, the issue was referred to a subcommittee of 10 (after lengthy arguments about how to get an appropriate balance between the two sides), which was charged with the difficult task of formulating a consensus statement on the subject. That committee eventually came up on the final day with the anodyne formula: 'Colonialism in all its manifestations is an evil which must be brought to an end.' Zhou Enlai had argued for the word 'manifestations' rather than 'forms', on the ground that it had significantly different implications and did not refer to the situation in Eastern Europe.

TATSUNOSUKE TAKASAKI (1885–1964)
MINISTER OF STATE AND DIRECTOR-GENERAL OF JAPAN'S ECONOMIC COUNCIL

The oldest head of delegation at Bandung, Takasaki kept a low profile and was one of the least voluble. A Japanese could hardly have behaved otherwise in an Asian gathering at that early stage of Japan's recovery from the World War II losses and damage.

Takasaki had spent the years of 1940–47 in Manchuria at the head of Manchuria Heavy Industries, during the years of Japan's wartime victories and ultimate defeat. He had previously been a director of various large business enterprises engaged in the production of iron, steel machinery and aircraft between 1917 and 1940. (No other delegate at Bandung had a remotely comparable record of business experience.) He became an advisor to the powerful Ministry of International Trade and Industry in 1952 and a cabinet minister in 1955.

The debate on colonialism and peaceful coexistence

The Political Committee turned to another controversial agenda item, 'promotion of world peace and cooperation', which gave rise to a 'second great discussion...[of] the questions of aligned versus non-aligned, *Panch Shila* and peaceful coexistence, war and peace'. Although nothing as dramatic as the Kotelawala outburst arose out of it, the discussions brought to the surface deep divisions among the delegates which proved difficult to resolve, even by the well-worn device of referring them to a smaller drafting committee to find a form of words that would paper over the differences between them all.

Fortunately, by this stage of the conference, no one really wanted to incur the odium of causing it to fail. It was agreed that it would have to be extended into Sunday, even though the Muslim holy month of Ramadan would have begun by then. And although that session was scheduled to end at 3 pm, it was in fact not until nearly three hours later that the Political Committee's formulating subcommittee on world peace and cooperation was able to reach consensus, after a lengthy and torrid debate. That meant it was nearly 10.30 pm—far behind schedule—before the conference finally wound up after all the concluding speeches.

The most difficult discussion, according to Abdulgani, arose over the two issues of the Five Principles of peaceful coexistence (*Panch Shila*) and the question of collective security pacts such as SEATO and CENTO (the Baghdad Pact). Iraq, Turkey, Thailand, the Philippines and Pakistan were again the strongest exponents of such collective security pacts, with Pakistan arguing the case most sharply. On the other side, India, Burma, Indonesia, Egypt and China put the case for 'peaceful coexistence', with support from Cambodia, Liberia and, somewhat surprisingly, Japan.

Mohammed Ali repeated what he had said earlier about the need

This terrible war [WWII] had been fought for the defence of Human Rights and the liberation of oppressed peoples. So it was natural for us to hope that now the time has arrived to feel secure and to work for peaceful development… However those hopes and aspirations were soon to be destroyed. The countries of Eastern Europe which had suffered under the ruthless oppressors again lost their independence—this time to a country which had entered their territories as liberators… Turkey also had to face ambitions directed against its independence and integrity. Hard pressure was exercised on us to make us cede part of our territory and to force upon us conditions incompatible with our national sovereignty and independence…

After these events the necessity of a united front for the legitimate defence of the independence and liberties began to take shape in the minds of the freedom-loving peoples… The right of self-defence, the right of peoples to unite their efforts for self-preservation and defence are natural and inalienable rights which are universally accepted and have been consecrated in the Charter of the UN…

These are the reasons and conditions which gave birth to the defensive alliance of peace-loving countries named NATO.

The same reasons, the same determination to resist aggression and defend peace, brought about the Balkan Pact, the Turkish-Pakistani Treaty of Friendly Collaboration, the Turkish-Iraqi Pact, the Southeast Asian Treaty Organisation, and other similar agreements.

It was [only then]…that hesitation began to be seen in the aggressive camp in the prospects of unleashing a 'shooting war' and the word 'coexistence' began to be used in their ranks.

– Turkish delegate

FATIN RUSTU ZORLU (1910–1961)
DEPUTY PRIME MINISTER OF TURKEY; MINISTER OF STATE

Educated at Istanbul, Geneva and Paris (Law, Finance and Political Science), Zorlu served in the Ministry of Foreign Affairs since 1932, and was posted to Geneva, Paris, Moscow and Beirut. One of the more experienced diplomats at Bandung, he was strongly anti-communist and pro-NATO. He was executed, along with other senior ministers, after a coup in 1960.

for two further principles to be added to the *Panch Shila* to create 'Seven Pillars of Peace'. His two additional principles were: 'the right of self-defence, exercised singly or collectively', and the obligation to 'settle all international disputes by peaceful means, namely negotiation or arbitration' (a dig at India over Kashmir). Jamali of Iraq supported him and Zorlu of Turkey was even sharper in his scepticism about the term 'peaceful coexistence', arguing that 'it is very naïve to believe that world peace can be maintained without a system of collective defence like NATO', which he and others claimed was essentially defensive in character.

The Indonesian foreign minister, Sunario, replied that peaceful coexistence was essential because the nations of Asia and Africa needed peace; but it must not be a peace based on a balance-of-power principle,

Europe has been in the past a continent full of conflict, full of trouble, full of hatred, and their conflict continues, and their wars continue, and we have been dragged into their wars because we were tied to their chariot wheels. Now, are we going to continue to be dragged in, and tie ourselves to Europe's troubles and Europe's hatreds and Europe's conflicts?

– Nehru

as seen by the great powers, for that gave rise to cold war, which might soon explode into a world war. Instead, Indonesia considered the Five Principles of coexistence essential. Nasser expressed general agreement with the idea of peaceful coexistence but added his own rather different set of seven principles, making a call for reduction of all armaments and armed forces, along with the elimination of nuclear weapons. Zorlu responded by reiterating Pakistan's insistence on the right of collective self-defence, arguing that in order to coexist, countries must be able to defend themselves and that without collective self-defence arrangements, Turkey would have lost her independence.

At this point, Nehru virtually 'exploded' with a 'sharp and rather intemperate' attack on the pro-Western group of countries, one of his longest and toughest speeches at the conference. Another world war would be catastrophic for the poorer nations, he insisted, and must be avoided at all costs. The nations of Asia and Africa could not prevent it, but they could help to lessen the tensions that might give rise to it. They must make it clear that they would not join either bloc.

If all the world were to be divided up between these two big power blocs… the inevitable result would be war. Therefore every step that takes place in reducing that area in the world which may be called the *unaligned area* [Nehru's emphasis] is a dangerous step and leads to war.

If a larger area of peace were to be created, the risk of war would be reduced, said Nehru. He then attacked the doctrine of collective defence, arguing that

every pact has brought insecurity and not security to the countries which
have entered into them. They have brought the danger of atomic bombs
nearer to them than would have been the case otherwise.

He described NATO as a powerful defender of colonialism, standing
in the way of the emancipation of Morocco, Tunisia and Algeria from
colonial rule. While he conceded that the Five Principles of the *Panch
Shila* were 'not a magic formula which will prevent all the ills of the
world', he asserted that they could help to lessen tensions. Moral force
does count, he asserted, and the Asian and African nations must exert
moral force, not become mere camp followers.

Nehru's speech evoked strong rejoinders from the pro-Western group.
Some stressed that the great difference between India's size and theirs
meant that they could not afford to stand alone and must unite with
others to ensure their security. Charles Malik of Lebanon reminded
Nehru that more than half the countries attending the conference were
linked to one or other of the two blocs by various pacts and they
presumably knew better than Nehru what was good for their own
security. Jamali of Iraq asked if Nehru was prepared to bring them all
together as a third bloc to give them the protection they needed (to which
Nehru replied that the time was not yet suitable for that, and that in any
case, such a bloc would involve its members in a common danger).

Zhou Enlai with members of
the Chinese delegation to the
Bandung conference.

Zhou Enlai stepped in again at this point to bridge the widening gap
between India and the Western-aligned states by waving an olive branch
which skilfully deflected the debate in another direction. If the term
'peaceful coexistence' was so objectionable because it was much used by
the communists, it could be dropped, he suggested. Why not simply
replace it with the words 'live together in peace', as used in the Preamble
to the UN Charter? He then turned to the Five Principles of peaceful
coexistence and urged that if some delegations could not fully agree with
them, they could be reformulated, added to or subtracted from to make

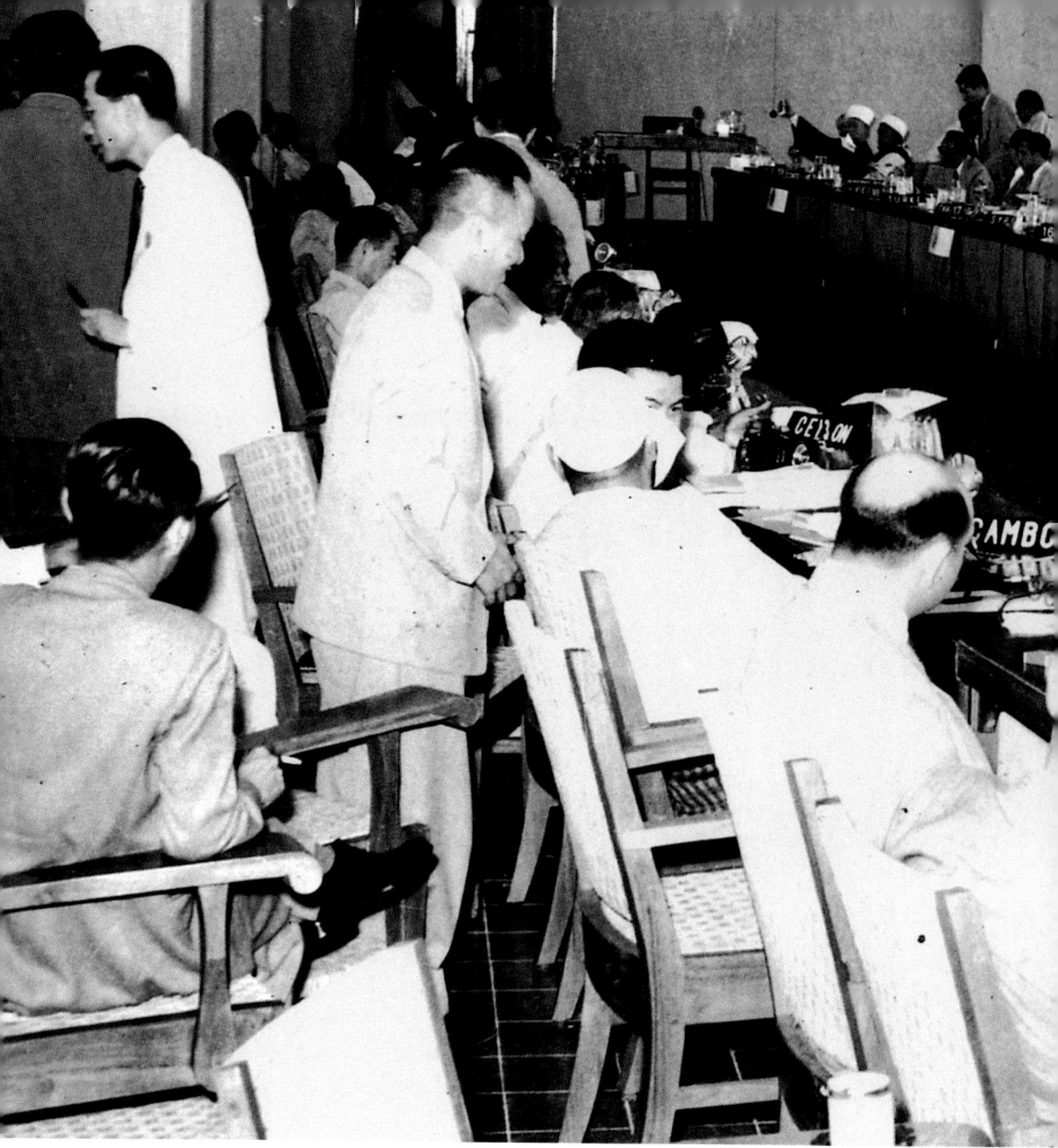

The Political Committee in session, the scene of some heated debates.

them acceptable to all delegates. He had his own list of seven principles which he then proceeded to spell out. But while that proved to be a useful contribution towards ending the deadlock—and a major step towards ultimate agreement on the Ten Principles of the *Dasa Sila Bandung* (rather than just the *Panch Shila*)—vehement debates on these issues continued over the next two days, almost wrecking the conference at the eleventh hour.

Last-minute dramas

At the end of an inconclusive debate on Saturday of peaceful coexistence,
a drafting committee was set up with Nasser as chairman and the highly
experienced Prince Wan as rapporteur. The Political Committee then
turned to the question of which Asian and African countries should be
recommended to the UN Security Council for acceptance as members of
the UN, where a tit-for-tat game of mutual vetoing by the two Cold War

camps was customary. On the basis of the principle of universality, it was recommended that countries participating in the AA Conference, such as Cambodia, Ceylon, Japan, Jordan, Libya, Nepal and 'a unified Vietnam', should be accepted as members.

The wording for Vietnam created controversy and several amendments, since it was necessary to find suitable words in accordance with the Geneva Accords and acceptable to both sides; but the delegate of the State of Vietnam (the anti-communist South) objected strongly, protesting against any reference to the Geneva Accords since his government had not signed them and rejecting the term 'unified Vietnam'. He also, in passing, accused India of 'taking sides' as Chair of the International Control Commission, provoking an outburst of anger from Nehru and a confused debate on what the phrase 'unified Vietnam' should mean, involving among others Pham Van Dong, Sihanouk and Zhou Enlai, who had all been involved in the Geneva negotiations. But they did not want to reopen an issue that had been regarded as adequately settled there a year before. So the issue was dropped by default and no mention of Vietnam was made at all in the final conference communiqué, an anomalous omission in view of the 1954 origins in Colombo of the idea for an AA Conference.

PRINCE WAN WAITHAYAKON KROMMUN NARADHIP BONGSPRABANDH (1891–1976)

FOREIGN MINISTER AND PERMANENT REPRESENTATIVE OF THAILAND TO THE UN

Educated at Balliol College, Oxford, and in Paris, Prince Wan joined Thailand's Foreign Ministry in 1920. He served as under-secretary of state for foreign affairs from 1924 to 1926, then as ambassador to London, Brussels and The Hague, and as head of delegation to the League of Nations in 1928. He was the prime minister's adviser and foreign minister from 1933 to 1946, and permanent representative to the UN since 1947. He was one of the oldest and most experienced of all diplomats at Bandung.

By Sunday afternoon, there was still no report of agreement from the drafting committees on either colonialism or peaceful coexistence, although the Economic Committee and the Cultural Committee had already submitted their consensus documents to the key Political Committee, made up of the heads of delegations. By 3 pm, the situation was still tense in both the deadlocked committees, while the press and public were waiting anxiously in the Gedung Merdeka for some word of the situation. Abdulgani phoned through from the Gedung Dwi-warna where the committees were meeting, with the approval of the conference chairman, Ali Sastroamidjojo, to say that the final plenary session would have to be postponed for an hour or two.

At 4 pm, Roeslan visited the colonialism subcommittee and learned, to his immense relief, that progress had been made, as Zhou had agreed to accept a compromise wording about the condemnation of colonialism 'in all its manifestations', rather than 'aspects'. (Zhou was later to tell the People's Congress in Beijing that it meant something entirely different, hence did not apply to the Soviet's position in Eastern

PRINCE NORODOM SIHANOUK (1922–)
KING OF CAMBODIA 1941–55, 1975–2004; HEAD OF GOVERNMENT 1955–70

A mercurial and erratic political actor, but constantly dedicated to keeping Cambodia from being dominated by the French or Americans (or overrun by the Vietnamese—he was uneasy about a Vietminh victory over the French in the early years), he became inclined towards neutralism in the 1960s.

He abdicated in favour of his father in 1954 to become Head of Government and leader of the Sangkum, the political party he created. He was overthrown by Lon Nol in 1970 with US backing. After the Pol Pot regime displaced Lon Nol in 1975, he joined forces with Pol Pot, surviving rather tenuously as king (although residing in Beijing and North Korea for much of the time, a characteristically unusual procedure) until he abdicated finally in 2004.

Seated from left to right: U Nu, Mohammed Hatta, Sukarno, and Ali Sastroamidjojo.

Europe.) But when he went on to the Nasser subcommittee on the wording of the 'peaceful coexistence' clause, he found that there had been no change of ground on either side. A proposal by Nasser that the right of collective self-defence be accepted, provided it not be used to serve the interests of the big powers, had been rejected, so he was losing hope of finding an acceptable form of words. Some delegates were already packing up their bags and preparing to leave the room when Roeslan intervened to urge them not to go until he had called the conference chairman to make a final effort to resolve the matter. He then left to summon Ali. The latter's account of what followed catches the last-minute urgency of it all:

As the time for the final session drew closer there was still no word from the committee by 4 pm and everybody was becoming increasingly restless. At about 4.30 pm, Roeslan Abdulgani reported to me that there was still no report from Nasser's committee

I immediately adjourned the meeting [of the Political Committee] and rushed to the ad hoc committee to find out for myself what stage the discussions had reached… I was shocked to see that they were all starting to put their papers and documents into their briefcases. When I asked why they appeared to be breaking up, the reply was: 'Deadlock!' Understandably I became very worried…and I urged them to try once more and not give up so quickly. I appealed to them, 'The success of the conference depends on you alone! I hope that you all will exercise mutual tolerance in our common interest, the interest of Asia and of Africa.'

The papers were taken out of the briefcases, he tells us, and the discussions were recommenced. 'I spoke to Prince Wan and asked that as rapporteur he assist the committee in trying to reconcile the various viewpoints…because I knew him to be a wise and experienced statesman'. When Ali returned to the Political Committee, he found the

atmosphere there had also become very tense.

Ali Sastroamidjojo chairing a session at the conference. He is flanked by U Nu, Sir John Kotelawala and Mohammed Ali, representatives of the other sponsoring nations.

> There was a general feeling of apprehension… But when asked how the work of the committee was proceeding, I tried to answer as calmly as possible, 'Oh, they will come up with a final statement within 30 minutes.' But the 30 minutes became an hour and a half… [Then] the committee entered and Nasser announced that its work had been completed.

The committee had agreed to accept the formula Nasser put forward earlier which it had previously rejected.

The final communiqué of the Bandung conference was then read by Prince Wan from the muddled notes of the proceedings he and Roeslan Abdulgani had been able to gather together. Its most important section consisted of the 10 articles which became known as the *Dasa Sila Bandung*, or the Ten Bandung Principles. A striking feature of these is that they do not mention the Nehru–Zhou *Panch Shila*, or look at all like them, or even the various sets of Seven Principles advanced by Mohammed Ali, Nasser and Zhou Enlai, but are an amalgam of diverse parts of them. Clauses 6 and 8 read quite differently from the others, as hard-fought clauses of this kind often are—a clue to bitter struggles over those issues. But consensus had been achieved, and in the circumstances, that was the most important thing.

After the draft communiqué was approved by the Political Committee, with only a few small alterations, Ali closed the session and

> we all rushed to the Freedom Building, where hundreds of people were patiently waiting to witness the closing of the conference, which was already two hours behind schedule… Roeslan Abdulgani read the as yet untyped final communiqué and after each head of delegation had delivered his final oration, I officially closed the conference with a short closing speech.

Such was the process of achieving the consensus reached at Bandung. Its meaning lay less in the words of the *Dasa Sila Bandung* or the much longer final communiqué—which was a mixture of worthy but rather unremarkable sentiments—than in the very fact that it had been possible to hammer together an acceptable statement at all. Without it the conference would have been judged a failure. With it, a glittering success could be claimed.

DASA SILA BANDUNG

The Ten Bandung Principles, as conveyed in the final communiqué of the conference, were as follows:

1. Respect for fundamental human rights and for the purposes and principles of the Charter of the United Nations.

2. Respect for the sovereignty and territorial integrity of all nations.

3. Recognition of the equality of all races and of the equality of all nations large and small.

4. Abstention from intervention or interference in the internal affairs of another country.

5. Respect for the right of each nation to defend itself singly or collectively, in conformity with the Charter of the United Nations.

6. (a) Abstention from the use of arrangements of collective defence to serve the particular interests of any of the big powers.
   (b) Abstention by any country from exerting pressures on other countries.

7. Refraining from acts or threats of aggression or the use of force against the territorial integrity or political independence of any country.

8. Settlement of all international disputes by peaceful means, such as negotiation, conciliation, arbitration or judicial settlement as well as other peaceful means of the parties' own choice, in conformity with the Charter of the United Nations.

9. Promotion of mutual interests and cooperation.

10. Respect for justice and international obligations.

TIMELINE: THE WEEK IN BANDUNG

Sat–Sun, 16–17 April
Delegations start arriving.
Preliminary unofficial meeting. Protest later by Pakistan.

Mon, 18 April
Official opening in public session.
Sukarno's opening address.
Procedural rules adopted.
Opening speeches in public session by delegates.

Tue, 19 April
Opening speeches continue.
Zhou Enlai's supplementary comments.

Wed, 20 April
The three committees meet in closed sessions.
Political Committee discussion of human rights and colonies.

Prince Faisal with a member of the Saudi Arabian delegation.

Thu, 21 April
Political Committee discussion of decolonisation.
Sir John Kotelawala's attack on Soviet 'colonialism' in Eastern Europe. Zhou demands right of reply.

Fri, 22 April
Zhou mollified. Political Committee discussions of 'peaceful coexistence'.
Major speeches by Nehru and Zhou.

Sat, 23 April
Debate continues. Tensions increase. Conference extended into Sunday.
Ad hoc committees meet to seek consensus formulae.
Ali Sastroamidjojo's lunch, resulting in Zhou's press statement offering a peaceful settlement of the Taiwan issue.

Sun, 24 April
Continued deadlock in the drafting committees stretches into late afternoon.
Final compromise reached around 6 pm.
Concluding speeches: conference ends at 10.30 pm.

Mon, 25 April
Delegations leave Bandung. Zhou visits Sukarno in Jakarta.

The large Indonesian delegation to the conference.

TROUBLED AFTERMATH:
AFRO-ASIAN SOLIDARITY CRUMBLES, 1955–1965

The Bandung conference and its Ten Principles (*Dasa Sila Bandung*) inevitably meant different things to different people. Afro-Asian solidarity and non-alignment were two of the key ideas emerging from it which came to be interpreted in strikingly divergent ways over the course of the next decade. Non-alignment gained increasing support among the newly independent countries of Africa, which became much more numerous in the early 1960s, while the 1961 Belgrade Conference of Non-Aligned Nations started to give it institutional form for the first time. But AA solidarity and the 'Bandung spirit' came under serious strain in those years. The divisions that arose were no longer between an aligned and non-aligned camp, as at Bandung, but were among diverse groups of the non-aligned themselves, with sharply differing views on what the goals of the Non-Aligned Movement (NAM) should be.

Sukarno in 1965 at the Indonesian Embassy in Rome.

Disputes, antagonisms and even wars between them contributed to the erosion of AA solidarity, especially the Sino-Indian border war of 1962. So too did the Sino-Soviet rift, which gave rise to diverse views of what either AA solidarity or non-alignment meant in the fast changing international order of the 1960s. The shift from the sharply divided bipolar world of the mid-1950s to the more fluid multipolar world of the 1960s, especially after the Sino-Soviet split opened up publicly around 1960–61, meant that non-alignment no longer signified what it did at Bandung. Non-alignment between whom, in such a world? 'If an attitude of non-alignment made any sense for most of the Afro-Asians in 1965,' wrote two Australian observers, a bit condescendingly, 'it was non-alignment between Russia and China'.

There is a significant recommendation…adopted without hesitation…that the Asian-African Conference should meet [again] at the proper time and place after consulting with the participating countries… This is a recommendation of paramount importance… We are not at the end, we are only at a beginning… We declare to the world that we [will] continue to meet, to assemble, to deliberate, to pool our combined will and efforts and resources until we see every degree of colonialism and imperialism washed [away] and destroyed for ever.
– Syrian delegate

The years 1955–65, between Bandung and the abortive second AA Conference in Algiers, were marked by two trends of great importance to the members of the group. The non-aligned nations increased greatly in numbers and political significance, mainly in Africa in the early 1960s, and the NAM thereby gained greatly in voting strength and visibility in the UN. Conversely, AA solidarity crumbled disastrously, for a variety of reasons. One was that a communist China could not, by definition, become a member of the NAM, so she had to rely on a revival of the 'Bandung spirit' and the support of Sukarno (who had reasons of his own, to which we will return shortly, to align with China after 1961), whereas India, who was by then seriously in conflict with China and Pakistan, was leaning towards Russia for political and military support, even to the point of backing her bid to become a fully-fledged participant in any further AA gathering. Hence there was a deep rift among the old Bandung partners over the central question of who should or should not be invited to a second AA meeting.

This made it almost impossible to conjure up the 'Bandung spirit' again as its 10th anniversary approached. 'The star which had risen in the political firmament of the Afro-Asian countries at Bandung did not shine brightly for long,' remarked Kimche. Yet the rhetorical appeal of Bandung as a symbol of unity still persisted within both the NAM and the very radical AAPSO (Afro-Asian Peoples' Solidarity Organisation, based in Cairo under Nasser's sponsorship), deeply divided as it was over the Sino-Soviet rift after 1960, which henceforth came increasingly into prominence.

Although reference had been made in the Bandung communiqué to a further meeting of the AA countries, no organisational arrangements or mechanisms had been set up (Nehru regarded this as superfluous),

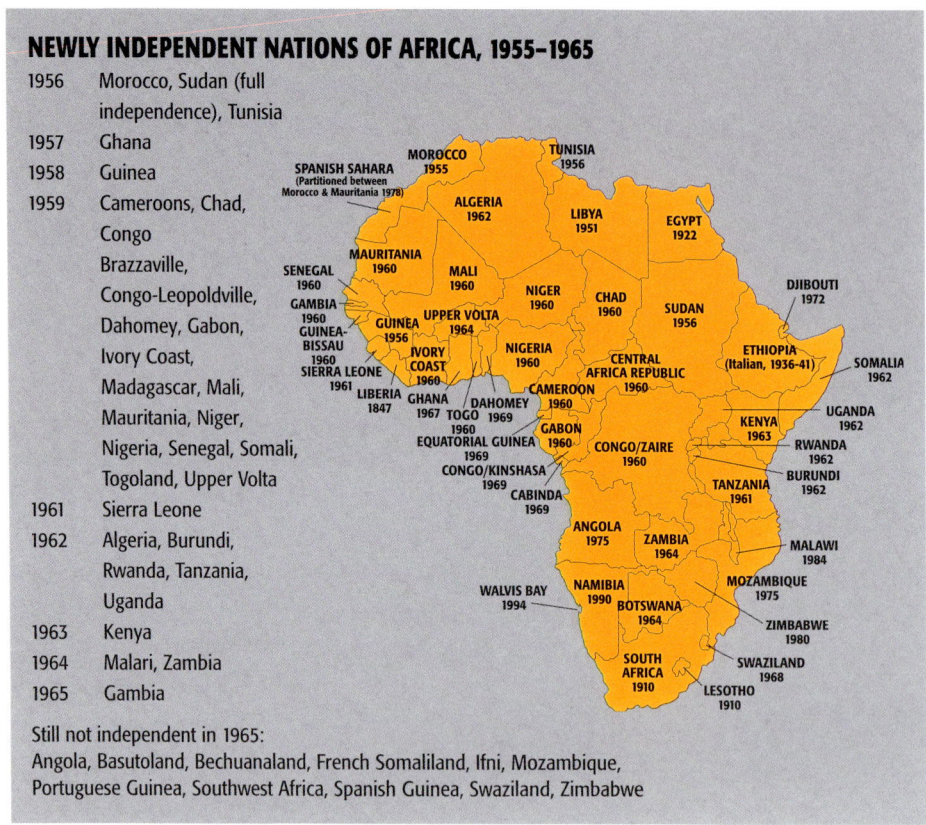

NEWLY INDEPENDENT NATIONS OF AFRICA, 1955–1965

1956	Morocco, Sudan (full independence), Tunisia
1957	Ghana
1958	Guinea
1959	Cameroons, Chad, Congo Brazzaville, Congo-Leopoldville, Dahomey, Gabon, Ivory Coast, Madagascar, Mali, Mauritania, Niger, Nigeria, Senegal, Somali, Togoland, Upper Volta
1961	Sierra Leone
1962	Algeria, Burundi, Rwanda, Tanzania, Uganda
1963	Kenya
1964	Malari, Zambia
1965	Gambia

Still not independent in 1965:
Angola, Basutoland, Bechuanaland, French Somaliland, Ifni, Mozambique, Portuguese Guinea, Southwest Africa, Spanish Guinea, Swaziland, Zimbabwe

and no action was taken to do so, although a few calls for it were made from time to time. During the Suez crisis of 1956, a meeting of the Indian, Burmese, Ceylon and Indonesian leaders was held in November, but little came of it, and the failure of the AA group as a whole to exert any pressure on Egypt's behalf underlined how little influence it could wield on an issue which should have had great relevance to it.

The Belgrade Conference 1961 and the birth of the NAM

The first of the meetings which gave rise to the NAM was held in Belgrade in September 1961 at the instigation of Nasser and President Tito of Yugoslavia, who were now collaborating closely on foreign policy issues. Nehru and Sukarno were there too, but were no longer so influential. The focus was far more on the threats to world peace then looming over Berlin than on colonialism or Afro-Asian problems. The

*[The Belgrade NAM conference was]
Bandung without China and with the
addition of Yugoslavia and Cuba.*
– Miller, Politics in the Third World

meeting represented a significant extension of the non-aligned group beyond its initially small Bandung family of primarily Asian and a few African nations. It was, wrote Miller, 'Bandung without China and with the addition of Yugoslavia and Cuba'. Only 15 of the 29 Bandung participants bothered to attend the Belgrade meeting. Later, the NAM grew greatly in size to include not only Cuba but also several other Latin American countries, as well as two European ones, Yugoslavia and Cyprus. More significantly, it led to the creation of an institutionalised and enduring movement, with a second Non-Aligned Summit meeting held in Cairo under Nasser's leadership in 1964, then others at fairly regular intervals thereafter.

Any hopes that NAM might become a vehicle for reviving the 'Bandung spirit' and Afro-Asian solidarity were wrecked, however, by the tangled international politics that began to develop in Asia and Africa in the following years, along with some bitter personal rivalries that arose. Ironically, all this happened at the very time when independence was being conceded to most of the British and French colonies in Africa. Calls to hold a second AA Conference as well as a second NAM meeting gave rise to intense controversies and rivalries.

Calls for a second AA Conference began to be made soon after the Belgrade meeting by Sukarno and several of the more radically anti-imperialist African leaders. Their motives then were far more diverse than in 1954–5 and the objectives to be achieved far less clear, at times little more than to apply diplomatic or political pressure on their rivals for leadership there. The NAM did not, by definition, include either China or the Soviet Union, so the Sino-Soviet rift which widened sharply around 1960–61 had less disruptive effects there than it did in the AA camp, into which Russia was pushing hard for acceptance, partly as a means of countering China's influence there. (Both were competing vigorously at that time for influence in the communist-front AAPSO.)

THE NON-ALIGNED MOVEMENT (NAM), 1961–2005

The Non-Aligned Movement came into being as a result of the Conference of Non-Aligned Nations which met in Belgrade, Yugoslavia, in September 1961, at the instigation (mainly) of Marshal Tito and General Nasser, at a time of acute international tension over the building of the Berlin Wall. It differed from the Bandung conference in several ways, most notably in having a formal structure, with a specific focus on and definition of non-alignment as its basis (whereas Bandung had an essentially geographical basis and no prior commitment to non-alignment at all), a continuing presence, as well as not being limited geographically to Asian and African nations. Invitations were sent to any countries that shared the aims and objectives of the proposed movement. It later came to include many Latin American countries and other small independent states from the Pacific and Indian Oceans, its numbers rising gradually from 25 in 1961 to 114 in 2004. But it has always acknowledged that its origins stem back not just to Belgrade but to Bandung also, and the principles enunciated there.

While Nehru and Sukarno were both present at Belgrade, leadership of the movement passed increasingly to Nasser and Tito. (Nasser had been impressed by the skill with which Tito had been able to defy pressure from Moscow since 1948 to conform to its demands upon all communist countries and eventually to win from President Krushchev in May 1955, soon after Bandung, a willingness to 'coexist' with Yugoslavia.) Nehru was by then in his twilight years, and preoccupied after 1962 with India's border conflict with China. Sukarno was trying hard to shift the stress in non-alignment towards a broader global conflict with imperialism and neocolonialism, appealing largely to the more radical leaders of the new African nations like Nkrumah and Sekou Toure. Nasser and Tito were less concerned than the Bandung leaders had been with issues of colonialism—by then a fading theme—and more with trying to mobilise the political influence of the Third World towards the prevention of conflict between the major nuclear powers, or to negotiating benefits for their own countries.

The criteria for membership of the NAM were adopted at a preparatory meeting in Cairo a few months before the Belgrade Summit. They were:

Heads of state at the 1961 Belgrade Conference (left) and at the 1992 NAM Summit in Jakarta (below).

1 The country concerned should have adopted an independent policy based on coexistence with States with different political and social systems and on non-alignment or should be showing a trend in favour of such a policy.

2 The country concerned should be consistently supporting the Movements for National Independence.

3 The country should not be a member of a multilateral military alliance concluded in the context of Great Power conflicts.

4 If a country has a bilateral military agreement with a Great Power, or is a member of a regional defence pact, the agreement or pact should not be one deliberately concluded in the context of Great Power conflicts.

5 If it has conceded military bases to a Foreign Power the concession should not have been made in the context of Great Power conflicts.

Since its inception, the NAM has 'attempted to create an independent path in world politics that would not result in Member States becoming pawns in the struggles between the major powers'. But in addition to that it has become increasingly focused on the need to restructure the international economic order, to promote South-South economic cooperation and to search for solutions to the widening gulf between the world's rich and poor nations.

It is noteworthy that by 2005, the NAM had grown to include Asian countries which at Bandung were opposed to the non-aligned group of countries because they were associated with security pacts such as SEATO and CENTO, notably Pakistan, Thailand, the Philippines and Syria, Lebanon and Iran. It also included three members of the communist bloc, Vietnam, North Korea and Cuba. But it did not include China or Russia, Turkey or Iraq.

Incessant wrangling therefore occurred among the non-aligned nations between 1963 and 1965 about who should or should not be invited to a second AA meeting. It proved a far more disruptive issue than anything that arose in 1954–5.

The problem boiled down essentially to the fact that India was by now supporting the Soviet Union's claim to be included, if and when such a meeting were held, on the basis of the Soviet Central Asian republics, whereas China was determined to keep her out. She was backed in this by Indonesia, who by 1964 needed China's support for her efforts to keep Malaysia out, on the ground that she was not truly independent, but merely a neocolonial puppet of the British. Isolating Malaysia from the AA family of nations became an increasingly dominant concern for Sukarno once the prospect of another AA Conference began to loom closer. But to ensure China's backing, he became strongly opposed to the inclusion of the Soviet Union. The logic and relevant factual bases of these wrangles were of secondary importance to the political alignments involved, but they took an inordinate amount of time and diplomatic activity throughout 1964–5.

There is no need to delve more deeply here into the tortuous negotiations that took place between the Belgrade Conference and the decision ultimately taken to hold a second AA Conference in Algiers in 1965. (It was generally agreed that it should be held in an African capital, and President Ben Bella, the first head of state of independent Algeria, was keen to have it there. Disastrously, however, he was overthrown by a coup only a few days before it was to begin, which led to a postponement that had fateful consequences.) Nasser was by this time playing a very prominent part in the complex politics of the newly independent African states, drifting away from his earlier close ties to Nehru and Sukarno as he developed his own notions of what non-

One of the last meetings between Mao and Khrushchev before the Sino-Soviet split.

NEUTRALISM AND NON-ALIGNMENT

Adherents to non-alignment frequently stressed that it was not the same thing as neutralism. The latter had a less favourable ring to it. Indian foreign policy was at first described officially as 'neutrality', then as 'dynamic neutrality', then it became 'neutralism' and later 'non-alignment'. By that was meant, according to Brecher, a Canadian biographer of Nehru, 'an active, dynamic, positive assertion of independent judgement on all issues, taking each on their merits, but maintaining freedom of action in international politics'. Non-alignment is 'a natural by-product of colonial subjection', observed Brecher. 'There is a psychological barrier to full fledged alliances with any bloc... which is equated with loss of freedom of action in external affairs. Indian leaders are intent on guarding their recently won freedom from all possible encroachments'.

Nehru himself preferred to use the phrase 'positive neutrality for peace', and at a time of dangerous Cold War tensions, he spoke much more of 'widening the area of peace' in Asia, as at Bandung, than of non-alignment per se. He refused to allow India to be harried into joining SEATO.

Mohammed Hatta, the vice-president of Indonesia until 1956, wrote similarly in 1953 that the 'active and independent' foreign policy of Indonesia *is not one of neutrality because it is not constructed with reference to belligerent states but for the purpose of strengthening and upholding peace. Indonesia plays no favourites between the two opposed blocs and follows its own path through the various international problems. It terms the policy 'independent' and further characterises it...as 'active'... It is not prepared to participate in any third bloc designed to act as a counterpoise to the two giant blocs. [It is not a policy of] neutrality which has a precise meaning in international law, defining a condition of impartiality towards belligerent states.*

Non-alignment was not widely accepted in Asia before Bandung (or even for several years after it), but made a strong appeal to Third World countries in the 1960s, after the formation of the NAM, largely under Nasser's and Tito's influence, initially. It was facilitated by the loosening up of the international system from the harsh rigidities of the early Cold War years after the death of Stalin in 1963, when Bulganin and Khrushchev began to shift their emphasis towards 'peaceful coexistence'. That widened the opportunities for the non-aligned countries to resist pressures from the great powers. It also meant that the rigidity of Dulles' hostility to non-alignment left the US opposed to the political tides of the late 1950s.

alignment meant. Nehru played less and less of a part in all this after the 1962 Sino-Indian War, and his death in early 1964 deprived India of its strongest spokesman there. Zhou Enlai was no longer China's foreign minister; in fact, his cordial post-Bandung policies towards China's neighbours were now being subordinated to the growing rivalry with the Soviet Union.

Sukarno's variation of non-alignment

A theme of particular interest in those events from an Indonesian angle, was the prominent part played by President Sukarno. In the early 1960s, he began to develop his own idiosyncratic idea of non-alignment, arguing against the conventional three-camp doctrine of a world divided

GAMAL ABDEL NASSER (1918–1970)

Egypt's premier, Lieutenant Colonel Nasser was not yet a widely known figure in international circles when he came to Bandung, nor did he play a very prominent role there, as he later did within the NAM. In fact, he was initially lukewarm about attending at all and he had to be persuaded to do so by Nehru. But Bandung 'appears to have affected him most strongly of all the participants', wrote Kimche, for his contacts with the Asian nationalist leaders, and with Zhou Enlai, 'opened new vistas in international relations and brought Nasser squarely into the camp of the militantly non-aligned, transforming the policy of non-alignment into the dominant trend of Africa and Asia'.

Nasser had risen to power in Egypt as the founder and leader of the 'Free Officers' secret organisation which overthrew King Farouk in 1952 and created the Republic of Egypt. In 1954, he displaced the elderly General Naguib as head of the Revolutionary Command Council and soon took over all the key military and political posts. He was strongly nationalist but by no means a democrat. He introduced a new constitution for Egypt in 1956 as a one-party, Islamic welfare state, and was elected president soon after with over 99 percent of the vote.

In 1956, he ordered the nationalisation of the Suez Canal to pay for the construction of the Aswan High Dam, after a US offer of funding for it was peremptorily withdrawn by Dulles. That led in due course to war with Britain, France and Israel, and a devastating defeat for Egypt's armed forces. Yet Nasser survived the defeat—as he also did in another disastrous war with Israel which he precipitated in 1967, the 'Six-Day War'—and became the foremost of all African leaders over the next 15 years, strongly anti-imperialist and a leading figure in the Non-Aligned Movement throughout the 1960s.

His rule was highly authoritarian and he utilised foreign policy as a means of buttressing popular support, striving to create a United Arab Republic through a merger with Syria in 1958 (which soon collapsed) but alienating the more conservative Arab rulers in the process. Yet as one of his foreign biographers has put it, 'this charismatic, almost mythogenic army officer…became the first true Egyptian to rule the country in several millennia, giving his people the dignity denied them under foreign rule.'

He died of a heart attack in 1970 at the age of 52.

between the two Cold War adversaries and the non-aligned, towards a more radical 'two-camp' theory, according to which the world was divided between the New Emerging Forces (NEF) and the Old Established Forces (of imperialism, neocolonialism and other 'reactionaries' to whom he was opposed, including even the Soviet Union at times). At the Belgrade Conference, he spoke of the conflict between 'the new emergent forces for freedom and justice and the old forces of domination', which derived from an inexorable clash between them and not just from an ideological difference, as Nehru, Nasser and

Tito were inclined to see it. He began to invoke the bogey of neocolonialism and imperialism more prominently, asserting also that they were the root cause of the world's conflicts, along with the forcible division of nations (an indirect reference to West Irian, as well as Taiwan, Vietnam, Korea and Palestine). By the time of the Cairo Conference of the Non-Aligned Movement, he was asserting that

> non-alignment must be anti-imperialist. If it is not anti-imperialist, then non-alignment is in reality already aligned, because it favours imperialism... [I]t is impossible to be 'non-bloc' as between imperialism and anti-imperialism or between the coloniser and those fighting the coloniser.

One of the reasons behind Sukarno's invocation of this new doctrine of the New Emerging Forces in conflict with the Old Established Forces was that it provided a very convenient ideological basis for his recourse to *Konfrontasi* against the newly formed state of Malaysia. This was a baffling mixture of actual armed attacks (but of a strikingly limited nature, largely symbolic and serving political rather than strategic purposes), threats, bluffs, propaganda and diplomatic pressures against her. But he also saw his NEF doctrine as having wider global implications, particularly as a means of mobilising support for resistance to the US (then becoming ever more deeply entangled in the Vietnam conflict) and its capitalist or neocolonialist allies.

As the 10th anniversary of the Bandung conference drew closer in 1964–5, Sukarno devoted an extraordinary amount of financial and bureaucratic resources to various mini AA conferences to highlight the

Marshal Josip Broz Tito (1892–1980), president of Yugoslavia, with Russia's Nikita Khrushchev (right) at Belgrade in 1955.

occasion and win international support for a second Afro-Asian Conference, partly as counter to the NAM. He had strong support from China in this, since she hoped to humiliate the Soviet Union and India by excluding the former from the Afro-Asian group, backed by the more radical (and now very numerous) African nations. Mao's belief in those days that 'the East Wind is prevailing' seemed to have some truth in it, and Sukarno certainly appeared to share it.

The Algiers conference

The circumstances of the second AA Conference in Algiers in 1965, however, proved to be utterly disastrous to the cause of Asian-African unity and solidarity. It was initially scheduled for June, but the Russians and Indians wanted it postponed, as they were not sure they could prevail there against the radical bloc led by China and Indonesia, both very eager to press ahead with it. The last-minute overthrow of Algerian President Ben Bella, followed not long afterwards by a bomb explosion in the conference hall at the last moment (which the new Algerian regime suspected was the work of the Egyptians, who were unhappy about Ben Bella's overthrow) provided a compelling excuse to postpone for several months.

It was then agreed to hold it in early November, but in the meantime, two dramatic developments occurred in Indonesia and China, radically changing the political balance in those countries and also in the wider Afro-Asian world. In Jakarta, the 30 September (*Gestapu*) coup attempt undermined Sukarno's political authority and his left-leaning government irrevocably, starting the swing to the right which brought General Suharto to power six months later. In China, Zhou Enlai's authority was being weakened by the early signals of the coming Cultural Revolution, so China's priorities too had to be switched to the domestic scene. Holding the Algiers conference suddenly became

把新老殖民主义者
赶出非洲去！

A 1964 Chinese propaganda poster, 'Expel the neocolonialists from Africa!', alluding to Soviet influence in some of the newly independent nations of Africa.

MEMBER STATES OF THE NAM IN 2005

not just a lower priority for both countries, but a serious embarassment, lest they find themselves outvoted.

Hence, when the preparatory meeting of foreign ministers assembled in Algiers late in October, shortly before the planned plenary meeting of heads of states, the boot was on the other foot. It was now China and Indonesia who wanted to avoid holding the conference, whereas India and Russia were eager to press on with it in the hope of swinging undecided votes their way. The conference hall was half-empty, with China, North Vietnam, Pakistan and several of the more radical African states notably absent. (Sukarno's government could hardly avoid participating, although only at the foreign minister level, as he himself was under too much pressure to leave Jakarta at that time.) The Algerian chairman defiantly declared that just as Bandung had been a starting point for the struggle for national liberation (a historically inaccurate assertion), Algiers must now become the same for the solidarity of all peoples struggling for peace.

US reconnaissance photo showing nuclear launch sites in Cuba during the Cuban missile crisis.

But with so few participants present, it was quickly decided not to proceed to a summit meeting of the heads of state; hence, the conference was indefinitely adjourned, never to resume. The second Afro-Asian Conference proved to be a non-event. 'Algiers has torn the mask off Afro-Asian solidarity, which is a myth and a farce', declared one Indian newspaper—a harsh judgment, but not an easy one to reject in those circumstances. The *Times of India* put it more cautiously, but aptly, 'the era opened by the Bandung Conference has come to an end'.

TIMELINE: THE AFTERMATH, 1955–1965

1956
- Crisis over Nasser's nationalisation of the Suez Canal.

1957–8
- Regional rebellions in Indonesia (PRRI-Permesta): Sukarno moves towards 'Guided Democracy', with the 'return to the 1945 Constitution' in August 1959.

1958–60
- China's 'Great Leap Forward'—an economic disaster.

1960
- Khrushchev, Nehru, Nasser, Sukarno and Castro attend UN General Assembly session.
- UN Resolution 1514 on the 'Ending of Colonialism'.
- Sino-Soviet rift widens.

1961
- 'Bay of Pigs' disaster for US President Kennedy in Cuba.
- Berlin Wall erected. Intensification of the Cold War.
- Belgrade Non-Aligned summit held (September).
- Indonesian political pressure in the UN against the Dutch to recover West Irian again fails.

1962
- Cuba crisis (October) threatens nuclear war.
- Sino-India border war.
- Sukarno intensifies military-diplomatic pressure on the Dutch to obtain West Irian.

The Suez Canal seen from the air.

1963–5
- Indonesian *Konfrontasi* ('Confrontation') of Malaysia. • China–Indonesia détente.
- 'Bandung vs. Belgrade' tussles over a 2nd AA Conference or 2nd NAM Conference.

1964
- Death of Nehru.
- Cairo Non-Aligned Conference held (October).

1965
- Indonesia quits United Nations (January).
- Sukarno summons various mini-conferences to celebrate 10th anniversary of Bandung and win support for 2nd AA conference.
- Algiers AA Conference in June aborted by overthrow of Ben Bella; it is postponed to November.
- *Gestapu* coup in Indonesia and start of Cultural Revolution in China change international political alignments radically.
- Algiers AA Conference in November collapses in disarray; it is adjourned indefinitely.

LOOKING BACK: JUST SYMBOLISM, OR SUBSTANCE TOO?

Fifty years on, what significance should we attribute to Bandung's historic gathering of Asian and African leaders? And what message does it hold for their successors, or the rest of the world, in today's very different circumstances?

It was at the time a very important symbol of the ending of the Vasco da Gama epoch of colonial dominance over the two continents, and it was seen as such for a few years afterwards, almost as the ritual final interment of the gloomy colonial past, experienced in varying degrees by virtually all the nations represented there (directly, in most cases; indirectly and mildly, in cases which had been quasi-colonies, like Thailand, perhaps China and others; or brutally, in the case of Africa's slave trade to America). The memories and hopes it raised began to fade, however, amidst the disastrous quarrels of the 1960s. So did it really amount to nothing more than that, a symbol? Simply 'words, words, words', as one acerbic Indian participant later dismissed it? (Though he himself had written unequivocally soon after the conference that, 'It was a success', because 'for the first time, it crystallised the greatest common measure of agreement among the Afro-Asian countries for the promotion of peace', showing 'realism and practicability' in the process.) Or did it have more enduring importance?

Jalan Braga in present day Bandung, with the Gedung Denis, another modernist building by A.F. Aalbers, who reshaped the Savoy Homann.

What did it achieve?

George Kahin, who had attended the conference as an observer, and knew the Indonesian leaders well, wrote soon afterwards that it had succeeded in achieving the aims of its sponsors—in fact, 'their expectations were more than fulfilled'—in that the sort of political environment they had hoped for was indeed created. He described that as one which would serve as a moral restraint against possible Chinese tendencies to aggression and would decrease significantly the danger of imminent war between China and the

US. He could have added that it helped to frustrate Dulles' aim of forcing the Asian nations to choose one side or the other on Cold War issues and to convince most of the world that there really was scope for a middle way between the polarities of the two main blocs. It greatly strengthened the appeal of non-alignment in many Asian societies. Its most enduring outcome was the NAM, which has continued to function until today and still looks back to Bandung as its true starting point. It partially helped to achieve Nehru's aim of 'widening the area of peace' by enhancing acceptance of the principle of peaceful coexistence and the *Panch Shila* (although less than he had hoped, according to some commentators).

It may not have done much towards softening the stony heart of Dulles, or changing the policies he had laid down for the US. But it did contribute to a significant shift in Soviet and Chinese policies towards the new states of Asia and Africa, as well as a softening of US policies towards them eventually, which occurred when Kennedy assumed the presidency in 1961. (Those shifts in turn gave rise to the Sino-Soviet rift, which became manifest after 1960 and profoundly transformed the global power balance.) In that respect, Bandung represented one of the first and most significant steps towards the emergence of a new multipolar world that developed later as the sharp polarities of the Cold War disintegrated.

President Sukarno welcoming delegates to the Bandung conference, 1955.

The NEFO batik, created by a radical supporter of Sukarno, dedicated to Asian-African solidarity and the struggles of the New Emerging Forces by incorporating an Indonesian *banteng* (wild bull), a Chinese dragon, a Middle-Eastern winged horse and an Afro-Asian elephant.
Collection National Gallery of Australia, Canberra.
Mohamad Hadi (1916–1983), Solo, Indonesia, NEFO, 1964, hand-drawn batik, cotton, natural dyes, 105 x 250 cm. National Gallery of Australia, 1984.3064.

A reassessment

At Bandung, the two ideals of non-alignment and Asian-African solidarity came together briefly and held out the hope of a brighter future after the dark years of the Cold War. But over the following decade, the trajectories of the NAM and the ideal of AA solidarity diverged seriously, as the fiasco at Algiers in 1965 revealed. That is cause for regret, but it does not negate the fact that the triumphant moment of convergence at Bandung in 1955 had both current political importance and broader historical significance. Memories of that kind can themselves be valuable to later generations, provided what we read into them will stand up to close scrutiny and searching criticism.

Memories and symbols can inspire, but they can also mislead. There are today various facile myths in circulation about Bandung as either a great success or a wordy failure. They need to be recognised as myths and brought into closer consonance with the truth about what actually happened there and what was achieved. That one week was an unprecedented and unrepeated moment of unity of purpose among the

nations represented there—and probably an unrepeatable one— brought about in a remarkable effort of will to fashion a consensus over the issues which could be agreed upon, while putting aside others at all costs, the inevitable requirement of con- sensus politics. The moment soon passed and the unity was in tatters by 1965, sadly, since it could not survive the tests of time and changing circumstances. Does that mean it was all just a chimaera, or was it something more than that?

Like other great moments in history—the post-1815 Concert of Europe, the Bismarckian power balance of the late 19th century, the euphoric optimism that attended the founding of the United Nations in 1945—that moment of Afro-Asian hopes and high ideals came and went. Hopes and ideals have their place in the conduct of world affairs, just as much as hard-headed Kissingerian realpolitik or the devious wiles of a Mao or a de Gaulle (curiously similar bedfellows in their resistance to hegemony by Moscow and Washington, as it turned out) or the rigid moralism of a Dulles. The ideals embodied in the florid rhetoric of Sukarno at Bandung, or Nehru's earnest reasoning for peace, or the pragmatic realism of Zhou Enlai in the business of reconciling opposites, may not have stood the tests of time as well as they and millions of others had hoped. But they did help to steer the world away from the nuclear war that the uncompromising self-righteousness of Dulles could easily have led to in the mid-1950s. And they did enable the differences between the aligned and non-aligned camps to be bridged at Bandung

The most important decision of the conference is the declaration on world peace and cooperation. The nations assembled set out the principles which should govern relations between them and indeed the countries of the world as a whole… [I]t would be a misreading of history to regard Bandung as an isolated occurrence and not part of a great movement of human history.
– Nehru, speech to Lok Sabha, *30 April 1955*

sufficiently to 'widen the area of peace' to some degree. (Cambodia, Laos and Jordan were early converts to it—and even Singapore, under Lee Kuan Yew in his early socialist, anti-colonialist phase.) Moreover, 'peaceful coexistence' came to be broadly accepted as something more than mere communist propaganda, and even as a necessary condition (indeed, an obvious one) for the avoidance of nuclear conflict.

No matter how limited the longer-term achievements of the Bandung conference may have been, they were far from trivial. And the conference did ensure that the call by the otherwise forgettable Sir John Kotelawala for 'Asia's voice to be heard' in an Asian international crisis made the impact it deserved. It was a big step away from the enforced silences that prevailed across Asia and Africa throughout the Vasco da Gama epoch. There have not been many such landmarks in the modern world.

Today, it is worth trying to see all this in its true perspective, without exaggerating it for rhetorical effect. That requires that we assess Bandung's significance in its historical context, in the light of the changing circumstances both of that time and today. It briefly held out the hope that in emerging from the dark night of the Vasco da Gama epoch, the new nations of Asia and Africa might be able to offer the world something to make it a better place. If the half-century celebrations of the Bandung conference (arranged under NAM's auspices in Jakarta and Bandung) can offer anything relevant to this day and age which can match that—a big call upon them—the expense could be well worthwhile.

Bandung today is no longer the gracious, charming place it was in 1955, but a rather shabby, overcrowded industrialising metropolis. The Gedung Merdeka and the grand hotels along Jalan Asia-Afrika are unlikely to inspire great visions for the future unless new ideas and new thinking are generated, as they were in 1955. But we must keep hoping that they can be found.

Towards a brighter future: a younger generation outside the renowned ITB (opposite).

NOTES & REFERENCES
A Brief Guide To Sources And Further Readings

Several official Indonesian government publications provide documentation on the official communiqué, opening and closing speeches in public sessions—but not the speeches and resolutions moved and either accepted or rejected in the closed committee sessions—and some have lists of conference delegates. The most accessible of these is *Collected Documents of the Asian-African Conference, April 18-24, 1955*, issued in 1983 by the Department of Foreign Affairs, Agency for Research and Development, Jakarta (cited below as *Collected Documents*). Several unofficial accounts have appeared, some of them based on access to the unpublished transcripts of committee proceedings, of which the most useful are by

George M. Kahin, 1956, *The Asian-African Conference. Bandung, Indonesia, April 1955*, Ithaca: Cornell University Press;

Roeslan Abdulgani, 1981, *The Bandung Connection. The Asia-Africa Conference in Bandung in 1955*, Singapore: Gunung Agung;

Christiaan L.M. Penders, ed., 1979, *Milestones on My Journey. The Memoirs of Ali Sastroamijoyo, Indonesian Patriot and Political Leader*, Brisbane: University of Queensland Press, pp 273–304 (cited below as Sastroamidjojo 1979);

Godfrey H. Jansen, 1966, *Afro-Asia and Non-Alignment*, London: Faber & Faber, ch. 8;

David Kimche, 1973, *The Afro-Asian Movement. Ideology and Foreign Policy of the Third World*, New York: The Halstead Press, ch. 3–5.

Kahin's account of the conference was the first and most informative in English (apart from a brief, India-oriented 1955 pamphlet by Appadorai). Other versions of it by Sastroamidjojo, Abdulgani, Kimche and Jansen are illuminating on various aspects.

CHAPTER 1

1. 'The voice of Asia'. A phrase derived from speeches by Sir John Kotelawala; see his 1956, *An Asian Prime Minister's Story*, London: George G. Harrap, pp 117–8.

2. Sukarno: 'This is the first intercontinental conference…' Printed fully in Kahin 1956, Abdulgani 1981 and *Collected Documents*.

3. Nehru: '…half the world's population'. From his speech to the *Lok Sabha*, New Delhi, 30 April 1955; see Nehru, *India's Foreign Policy: Selected Speeches 1946–81*.

4. 'This is the human race speaking…' Richard Wright, 1956, *The Color Curtain*, pp 9–12.

The End of the 'Vasco da Gama epoch'

5. K.M. Panikkar, 1953, *Asia and Western Dominance. A Survey of the Vasco da Gama Epoch of Asian History 1498–1945*, London: Allen & Unwin, pp 11–12.

Pan-Asianism and Pan-Africanism: Some Precursors

6. Nehru: 'India's exploitation…' Michael Brecher, 1959, *Nehru. A Political Biography*, London: Oxford University Press, p 111.

7. Nehru: 'An event of first-class importance…' Nehru told Brecher (1959:109) that the Bandung conference 'may be seen as the fruition of an idea that had first found expression at Brussels about thirty years earlier'.

8. Manchester Conference. Colin Legum, 1962, *Pan-Africanism. A Short Political Guide*, London: Pall Mall Press, pp 31–2.

Bandung… 'The coolest and nicest spot in Java'

9. 'The coolest and nicest spot in Java'. *Bandoeng Vooruit*, 1939, 'Bandoeng—A Holiday Wonderland', Bandung: *Bandoeng Vooruit*.

10. 'Bandung provided the ideal surroundings…' Arjun Appadorai, 1955, *The Bandung Asia-Africa Conference*, New Delhi: Indian Institute of World Affairs, p 5.

11. Bandung's architecture. Huib Akhari, 1988, *Architechtur en Stedebouw in Indonesie: 1870–1970*, De Walburg Pers, ch. 8–9. Haryono Kunto, 1991, *Wajah Bandung. Tempo Doeloe*, Bandung: P.T. Granesia.

Sukarno

12. 'A highly individual leader…' John D. Legge, 2003, *Sukarno: A Political Biography*, Singapore: Archipelago Press, pp 15–16.

CHAPTER 2

13. Nehru's objectives. Brecher 1959:588–9.

14. Ali Sastroamidjojo's domestic and foreign policy agenda. Herbert Feith, 1962, *The Decline of*

Constitutional Democracy in Indonesia, Ithaca: Cornell University Press, pp 384–6.

15. Dulles and the 'domino effect'. Stanley Karnow, 1984, *Vietnam. A History*, Penguin Books, pp 169–70. The term was first used in public by Eisenhower on 7 April 1954, according to Townsend Hoopes, 1974, *The Devil and John Foster Dulles*, London: Andre Deutsch, p 14.

16. The battle of Dien Bien Phu. Karnow 1984:555, 582–4.

17. US rejection of Zhou's offer. Abdulgani 1981:149–52; Sastroamidjojo 1979:300–301.

The Geneva Conference and Vietnam

18. 'We are here to re-establish peace, not to back the Vietminh'. Karnow 1984:201.

SEATO and CENTO

19. Dulles' call for 'united action'. Richard Goold-Adams, 1962, *The Time of Power: A Reappraisal of John Foster Dulles*, London: Weidenfeld and Nicolson, pp 134–7, 144–51.

Zhou Enlai

20. Nehru: 'Whenever he spoke…' Sarvepalli Gopal, 1979, *Jawaharlal Nehru: A Biography*, London: Jonathan Cape, p 241.

21. 'One of the most brilliant diplomats…' Karnow 1984:200.

John Foster Dulles: 'Neutralism is immoral'

22. 'The principle of neutrality… obsolete'. Hoopes 1974:314–7. Dulles wrote that the idea that a state can best gain safety for itself by being indifferent to the fate of others has become 'an obsolete conception… an immoral…and short-sighted concept' (*State Department Bulletin*, 18 June 1956).

23. 'Monumental self-righteousness…' Herman Finer, 1964, *Dulles over Suez*, London: Heinemann, p 51.

24. 'My offer is withdrawn.' Finer 1964:48.

25. Was he great or disastrous? Goold-Adams 1962:294 ff.

CHAPTER 3

26. 'What a chain reaction…' Kotelawala 1956:118.

27. 'Where do we nations of Asia stand now?' Sastroamidjojo 19/9:276.

28. 'The chance to put my proposal…' ibid. 277

29. 'Obvious diplomatic understatement…' ibid. 278

30. 'The personalities of my distinguished colleagues…' Kotelawala 1956:120.

31. Nehru's 'cautious and lukewarm attitude…' Sastroamidjojo 1979:281.

32. 'How different were the opinions…' Abdulgani 1981:23.

33. 'That obscene symbol of Dutch colonialism'. Legge 2003.

34. 'I decided on Bandung'. Sastroamidjojo 1979:283.

35. Nasser's reluctance to attend. Jansen 1966:183.

Sir John Lionel Kotelawala

36. 'The most undiplomatic diplomat…' Sastroamidjojo 1979:294.

Jawaharlal Nehru

37. Gandhi as 'India's most illustrious son'. Brecher 1959:58.

38. '…in the background, quiet, studied'. Wright 1956:141–2.

Ali Sastroamidjojo

39. A more 'active and independent' foreign policy. See Feith 1962:384–6 for the political background to that shift.

U Nu

40. U Nu, 1975, *Saturday's Son*, New Haven: Yale University Press.

CHAPTER 4

41. Mohammed Ali 'exploded' in anger. Abdulgani 1981:77.

42. Sukarno's opening address. *Collected Documents* 1983.

43. 'New colonialism' speeches. Kahin 1956.

44. Zhou Enlai's speech. Printed in full in Kahin 1956:14–15.

45. Zhou's 'modest and attractive' tone. Abdulgani 1981:107. Similar comments by Nehru can be found in Gopal 1979:241 and by Romulo in Carlos P Romulo, 1956, *The Meaning of Bandung*, Chapel Hill: University of North Carolina Press, p 11.

46. Romulo and Malik in the human rights debate. Roland Burke, 2004, 'The Compelling Dialogue of Freedom. Human Rights at the Afro-Asian Conference, Bandung, April 1955', paper presented to the Asian Studies Association of Australia

Biennial Conference, Canberra 2004.

47. 'Another form of colonialism…' Kotelawala 1956:186–8; Abdulgani 1981:114–18.

48. 'I granted Zhou's request'. Sastroamidjojo 1979:293; Abdulgani 1981:115–16.

49. Exchanges between Zhou, Sir John and Nehru. Kotelawala 1956:187–9; Sastroamidjojo 1979:294–5; Abdulgani 1981:117.

50. Zhou's reply on 'a new colonialism'. Sastroamidjojo 1979:296.

51. '…serious and disruptive deadlock'. The words are Kahin's, 1956:19.

52. 'A second great discussion…' Kimche 1973:70; Abdulgani 1981:137–48; Sastromidjojo 1979:297–9.

53. The most difficult discussion. Abdulgani 1981:181–4; Kahin 1956:21–32.

54. Nehru virtually 'exploded'. Kahin 1956:23–4; cf. Abdulgani 1981:140–44.

55. Zhou's alternative to 'peaceful coexistence'. Abdulgani 1981:146.

56. Reports of Economic and Cultural Cooperation committees. *Collected Documents* 1983:137–40; Abdulgani 1981:181–4.

57. Last-minute dramas. Sastroamidjojo 1979:287–8; Abdulgani 1981:157–62.

58. Final communiqué. *Collected Documents* 1983; Abdulgani 1981:181–90.

Katay Don Sasorith

59. An 'irrepressible' nationalist. Grant Evans, 2003, *A Short History of Laos. The Land in between*, Australia: Allen & Unwin; Martin Stuart-Fox, personal communication.

CHAPTER 5

60. 'If an attitude of non-alignment made any sense…' T.B. Millar and J.D.B. Miller, 1965, 'Afro-Asian Disunity: Algiers, 1965', *Australian Outlook*, xix, 3:310.

61. 'The star…did not shine brightly for long'. Kimche 1973:250.

62. Belgrade Conference as 'Bandung without China…' Kimche 1973:96, quoting J.D.B. Miller, 1967, *The Politics of the Third World*, Oxford University Press, p 33.

63. Tortuous negotiations. Kimche 1973:98–120.

64. New Emerging Forces. Frederick Bunnell, 1966, 'Guided Democracy Foreign Policy 1960–1965', *Indonesia*, no. 2, pp 37–76.

65. 'Non-alignment must be anti-imperialist…' Cited in J.A.C. Mackie, 1974, *Konfrontasi. The Indonesia-Malaysia Dispute 1963-1966*, Kuala Lumpur: Oxford University Press, p 97.

66. *Konfrontasi* and the NEF doctrine. Mackie 1974: 94–103, 276–92.

67. Algiers and Asian-African unity. Kimche 1973:118–23; Millar & Miller 1965:306–21; Guy Pauker, 1965, 'The Rise and Fall of Afro-Asian Solidarity', *Asian Survey*, vol. 5, no. 9, pp 425–32.

68. 'Algiers has torn the mask off…' Kimche 1973:122–3, quoting the *Indian Express* and *The Times of India*, both 3 November 1965.

Neutralism and Non-Alignment

69. India's 'active, dynamic' policy. Brecher 1959.

70. 'A natural by-product of colonial subjection'. Brecher 1959:558–61.

71. '…is not one of neutrality…' Mohammed Hatta, 1953, Department of Foreign Affairs publication, pp 441–52.

Gamal Abdel Nasser

72. Bandung 'opened new vistas…' Kimche 1973:82.

73. 'This charismatic, almost mythogenic army officer…' Robert St. John in Encyclopaedia Britannica (15th ed.), vol. 12, p 844–5.

CHAPTER 6

74. 'Words, words, words'. Arjun Appadorai 1971, 'The Bandung Conference in Perspective', *Essays in Indian Politics and Foreign Policy*, New Delhi: Vikas Publications, p 182. His 1971 assessment contrasts sharply with the very favourable assessment in Appadorai 1955:27–32.

75. 'Their expectations were more than fulfilled'. Kahin 1956:36.

76. NEFO batik. Mohamad Hadi (1916–1983), Solo, Indonesia, NEFO, 1964, hand-drawn batik, cotton, natural dyes, 105 x 250 cm, National Gallery of Australia, 1984.3064. A unique experiment in combining various Asian cultural symbols with the most traditional of Javanese art forms in order to convey a radical political message. For further details, see J.R. and R.J. Maxwell, 'Political Motives: The Batiks of Mohamad Hadi of Solo', in M. Grittinger, ed., 1989, *To Speak with Cloth: Studies in Indonesian Textiles*, Los Angeles: University of California, Museum of Cultural History.

INDEX

PICTURE CREDITS

While every effort has been made to trace copyright holders, in some cases this has proved impossible. The publisher of this book would be grateful to hear from any copyright holders not acknowledged.

Pictures not specifically credited below were generously provided by the Asian-African Conference Museum of Bandung. Other pictures are gratefully acknowledged to the following collections, owners and photographers: